PRA
LATTER-DAY WARRIORS

"This book will inspire you to be better, have more faith in Jesus Christ, and dig deeper in your efforts to serve Him. Brock captures the essence of faith when he shares his own stories of finding the strength to follow the Savior. Brock is a warrior who humbly invites us along to reconnect with Father in Heaven and stand firm and steadfast in our dedication to His Son Jesus Christ."

—**Chad Lewis,** Super Bowl champion, three-time NFL Pro Bowl selection, Ed Block Courage Award recipient, author of *Surround Yourself with Greatness*

"Brock Richardson's *Latter-Day Warriors* is a powerful description of the way some champion athletes not only excel in the arena of sports but also are champions in dealing with the toughest challenges of life. I strongly recommend this book to both young and adult readers who want to win in the battle of life."

—**Ron McMillan,** four-time *New York Times* bestseller, coauthor of *Crucial Conversations*

"This young man never ceases to amaze me. He took what little I taught him in the gym about football, lifting, and my life philosophies and made himself the best athlete and sportsman he could be. Outside of sports, Brock has used the same undying love and hard work toward his family and faith. I am so proud to call this young man my friend and brother. He has taught me more about belief and being a good man than I have ever taught him about sports and competition. Brock and the Richardson family have overcome some staggering losses since I have known them; not once did their devotion to their faith waver. They are what I believe the LDS faith is all about: pure love, pure family, and pure faith. This book is invigorating and will give you an undying warrior's spirit toward your faith."

—**Blaine Berger,** 1997 Muscle and Fitness NFL Strength Team with the Arizona Cardinals, 1996 NFL-Europe All-World Team, and three-year starting defensive tackle at the University of Utah

"A valuable read for youth! Channeling feelings correctly, taking a stand, prioritizing life through the lens of the gospel, summoning courage, building faith and testimony—all these subjects and more are eloquently addressed by Brock Richardson, an up-and-coming LDS author and seminary teacher. Someone who knows!"

—**Larry Barkdull,** author of
Rescuing Wayward Children and *Pillars of Zion*

LATTER-DAY
WARRIORS

BROCK LANCE RICHARDSON

LATTER-DAY
WARRIORS

STEPPING INTO YOUR SPIRITUAL STRENGTH

FOREWORD BY
BRONCO MENDENHALL

CFI
An Imprint of Cedar Fort, Inc.
Springville, Utah

This is not an official publication of The Church of Jesus Christ of Latter-day Saints. The opinions and views expressed herein belong solely to the author and do not necessarily represent the opinions or views of Cedar Fort, Inc. Permission for the use of sources, graphics, and photos is also solely the responsibility of the author.

ISBN 13: 978-1-4621-1705-5

Published by CFI, an imprint of Cedar Fort, Inc.
2373 W. 700 S., Springville, UT 84663
Distributed by Cedar Fort, Inc., www.cedarfort.com

LIBRARY OF CONGRESS CATALOGING-IN-PUBLICATION DATA

Richardson, Brock Lance, 1985- author.
Latter-day warriors : stepping into your spiritual strength / Brock Lance Richardson ; foreword by Bronco Mendenhall.
    pages cm
Interviews with ten Brigham Young University football players.
Includes bibliographical references.
ISBN 978-1-4621-1705-5 (perfect bound : alk. paper)
1. Spiritual life--Church of Jesus Christ of Latter-day Saints. 2. Christian life--Mormon authors. 3. Conduct of life. 4. Football players--Utah--Provo--Biography. 5. Brigham Young Cougars (Football team)--Biography. I. Mendenhall, Bronco, 1966- writer of foreword. II. Title.
BX8656.R53 2015
248.4'89332--dc23
                                    2015027442

Cover design by Shawnda T. Craig
Cover design © 2015 Cedar Fort, Inc.
Edited and typeset by Kevin Haws

Printed in the United States of America

10 9 8 7 6 5 4 3 2 1

Printed on acid-free paper

Dedicated to my father, Lance Melvin Richardson

"Ye shall know them by their fruits" (Matthew 7:16).

CONTENTS

FOREWORD

As the head football coach at BYU, I look into the eyes of a new crop of young players every season and I see similarities. I see strong, competitive young men who are gifted athletes with a passion to play football. And due in large part to these similarities, I also see a unique group of young men. There are more than a million high school football players in the United States, but of those only an elite few—less than 3 percent—will play Division 1 college football. These young men are part of that elite few.

We are excited for them to join our program—and work and learn alongside those who have come before them. They become part of our band of brothers. Our coaching staff invests all the resources we have into these individuals, teaching them our knowledge of the game, drilling them on plays, honing their techniques, and pushing them to their physical limits. The process is intense. Then, on game day, we take the field and together go to battle. It's a war on the field—these young men have to be warriors.

In addition to what takes place on the field, I also get the unique opportunity of being a part of something that is much bigger than the game of football. I get to help facilitate the growth of young men who will eventually become leaders in their homes, communities, and the world. They can become not only warriors on the field but also spiritual warriors in life. This, however, does not happen overnight. It is a process that unfolds as each young man shows willful obedience, hard work, and enthusiasm to the commitments that are asked of him.

Brock Richardson is one of these young men. Brock was responsible and accountable in all he did as a member of the BYU football program.

As I reflect on the many incredible young men who have been part of our program at BYU, I think the individuals Brock has chosen to highlight in this book are inspiring. They are examples of the most committed warriors who have risen to the challenge. Faith was their priority. Circumstance and setbacks were never an excuse to quit the pursuit. I'm proud to know each and every one of them. They, along with so many others like them, have changed my life.

—Bronco Mendenhall

ACKNOWLEDGMENTS

Special thanks to Matt Davis, Ron McMillan, and Bronco Mendenhall for being in tune enough with the Spirit to get the ideas of this book started. Thanks to the ten men and their wives who are highlighted in this book; their warrior stories inspired the deepest feelings of "warrior-hood" within me. My utmost appreciation goes out to Nate Meikle, Dixie Richardson, my family, and the editing team at the Church Department of Correlations—each and every one of their edits was insightful, well-thought, and helpful.

Most of all, thanks to Stephanie—the love of my life, the reason I am or ever will be a warrior. Thanks to my kids, Kinlee and Kade, who inspire me to keep reaching for personal warrior-hood every day.

THE LATTER-DAY WARRIOR IN YOU

Y ou've only been a member for a year?!" I was flabbergasted. Elder Barkle, one of Uruguay's most zealous missionaries, had been converted to The Church of Jesus Christ of Latter-day Saints only one year previous. *How could this be?* I thought to myself. For those of us missionaries who lived with him, he was an example of what it meant to be truly converted to the gospel of Christ. Down there in Paysandu, Uruguay, Elder Barkle never hesitated to run after people on streets or stand up on buses, literally shouting his testimony to those who hadn't heard of Jesus Christ.

"How did you get so dedicated in one year?" I asked him. He chuck-led, almost apologetically. "Oh, Elder Richardson, I'm just trying." He was so humble. It was almost strange to me how somebody so zealous out on the streets seemed to think nothing of himself in person.

I pressed on. "I mean, there must be some reason you're standing up on buses—some reason you get so emotional and fiery when bearing testimony and telling people about our message. What is it?" I yearned to have desire like he had. I craved knowing what could have caused such love for the gospel in so short a time.

"It started in Southern Cali, where I lived, in a history class at my high school. This girl stood up and said something at the end of class. I didn't know her very well, but what she said changed me forever."

What could a girl have possibly said that would have caused this surge of heartfelt testimony I see coming from Elder Barkle every day? I wondered.

"The lesson that day was about the 'Mormons' moving out West," he said. "I hadn't heard of Mormons before then, but the lesson gave them a bad look, focusing on some of the issues that they were hated for. After the lesson was finished, the girl stood up in front of everyone and told us we hadn't heard the full story about Mormons. She said that Mormons weren't really all that bad and if anyone had any questions about them we could just ask her.

"I didn't know exactly what happened to me," Elder Barkle continued, "but something like lightning shot through me. Up to that point, I hadn't been really interested in any church, but as soon as the bell rang, I walked right up to her to find out more about her church. I was so excited, and I didn't know why. 'I don't know what a Mormon is, but when you said that in front of everyone, something like electricity shot through me, so I need to know more,' I said. The rest is history. She invited me to mutual, then she invited me to church, and then I got baptized." He was so humble and simple about it, but when he told me his story, I felt that same bolt of lightning he must have felt in his history class.

It's now been about a decade since he told me his story, but it got me thinking. To this day, I don't even know that girl's name, or who she is. "Does that girl even know?" I have often asked myself. "Does she even know that Uruguay practically *exploded* with the testimonies of that zealous young man and that her courage to stand up contributed to that? Does she even know that she helped Uruguay find the joy, excitement, and enthusiasm of the gospel?"

A good friend once told me, "You can count the seeds in an apple, but you can never count the apples in a seed." When that girl stood up in a California history class, she planted something of a seed in Kameron Barkle's heart. She may never know that a book is now being written with one of her stories in it, but that's just one of the apples in the seed of her testimony that she'll never be able to count.

The thought of that girl, among other warrior-like souls like her, started this book. Joel, the Old Testament prophet, made a prophesy about youth of the latter days: "And it shall come to pass afterward, that I will pour out my spirit upon all flesh; and your sons and your daughters shall prophesy . . . your young men shall see visions: and also upon the servants and upon the handmaids in those days will I pour out my spirit. And I will shew wonders in the heavens and in the earth" (Joel 2:28–30). I'm pretty convinced that latter-day youth don't even begin to comprehend who they are or what a drastic change for good they can make.

> And there was war in heaven; Michael and his angels fought against the dragon; and the dragon and his angels fought against Michael; and the dragon prevailed not against Michael. . . . Neither was there place found in heaven for the great dragon, who was cast out; that old serpent called the devil, and also called Satan, which deceiveth the whole world; he was cast out into the earth; and his angels were cast out with him. . . . And after these things I heard [a] voice saying, Woe to the inhabiters of the earth, yea, and they who dwell upon the islands of the sea! for the devil is come down unto you, having great wrath, because he knoweth that he hath but a short time. (JST Revelation 12:7–12)

You're a warrior. You have already fought a tremendous battle against those who were opposed to Heavenly Father's plan—and you were victorious. The prophet Ezra Taft Benson spoke to us, the latter-day generation, when he said, "You are choice spirits, many of you having been held back in reserve for almost 6,000 years to come forth in this day, at this time, when the temptations, responsibilities, and opportunities are the very greatest" ("A Message to the Rising Generation," *Ensign*, November 1977). Think about it: You did something that qualified you to be called "choice"! What did you do?

Did you fight alongside other choice spirits, like Captain Moroni and the stripling warriors, or alongside David, who slew Goliath? With courageous women like Esther, Ruth, and Eve? This is not only possible; it's likely. And, if you fought alongside Captain Moroni, you may find within yourself some of his indomitable courage. What if you have some of that unyielding desire for liberty that Eve had?

What drove the warrior within you in that battle in heaven? Continuing in the Joseph Smith Translation of Revelation 12, verse 10 states, "They have overcome [the devil] by the blood of the Lamb, and by the word of their testimony." One of your greatest weapons was (and is) your testimony. You bore it with the conviction of a warrior and, through Christ, conquered the dragon. One difference, however, between you and those heroic figures mentioned before is that you have not yet finished the fight. They have completed their stories—they have lived out the last round of their battles. Yours remains to be written.

You were made with limitless potential. If you are truly dedicated to personal scripture study and prayer, you can have spiritual experiences that reveal who you truly are and who you are meant to become. Abraham had a special experience as he became close to the Holy Spirit: "Now the Lord had shown unto me, Abraham, the intelligences that were organized before the world was; and among all these there were many of the noble and great ones; and God saw these souls that they were good, and he stood in the midst of them, and he said: These I will make my rulers; for he stood among those that were spirits, and he saw that they were good; and he said unto me: Abraham, thou art one of them; thou wast chosen before thou wast born" (Abraham 3:22–23). This experience undoubtedly bolstered Abraham's confidence and helped him become who he was meant to become.

What about you? Will you have the courage to seek experiences with the Spirit that show who you were in premortal life, what you promised to do, and your mission in this life? You undoubtedly did *something* special in the premortal existence that qualified you to be "held back in reserve for almost 6,000 years." Exactly what you did, and exactly who you were chosen to be, can only be discovered in drawing near to the Holy Ghost, as Abraham did.

You don't remember fighting on the side of the Savior in the premortal existence, nor do you remember proving yourself as a leader—one who could help finish the fight against the devil. But Satan does. Many of his angels who fought against you know exactly who you were before your life here. They remember what you said or did and how hard you fought in order to triumph. They are terrified that you might step into that strength once again, so they desire to destroy the good within you. Knowing "that [they have] but a short time" (JST Revelation 12:12), they're determined to entice you to sin before you can have experiences like Abraham's and find out who you were before this life.

Satan often pretends to be your friend and slowly lulls you into complacency, into foregoing your warrior destiny. He will tell you, "There is no hell; and he saith unto [you]: I am no devil, for there is none—and thus he whispereth in [your] ears, until he grasps [you] with his awful chains, from whence there is no deliverance" (2 Nephi 28:22). In other words, he says, "There is no war because there never was a devil to fight against. You aren't a warrior." He knows that if you don't understand the fighting spirit within you, he's all the closer to winning.

But there *is* an ongoing spiritual war, even amongst us right now, and you *can* be a warrior for Jesus Christ. This present battle against hatred, jealousy, pride, disrespect, pornography, and lies against the truth (2 Timothy 3:1–7) is the same battle we began in the premortal existence. Satan surely has "come down unto you, having great wrath, because he knoweth that he hath but a short time" (JST Revelation 12:12). Merely sidestepping wickedness and temptation will not be enough anymore. As a true warrior of God, you were meant to open your mouth, bear your testimony, and openly defy the temptations that will come. You must revive that greatest weapon of old, the weapon of your testimony!

The Search for the Warrior within Myself

I'm on the same journey you are on, struggling to recognize the latter-day warrior in myself. During times of fear and doubt, I wonder if there ever really was a warrior within me. There are times, however, when I do feel a warrior emerging. It started ten years ago, and I still feel I have such a long way to go, but the story of how I discovered that warrior in myself may help you remember times when your own fighting spirit has emerged.

I grew up in Idaho Falls, Idaho. My dad and I were the best of friends. Instead of hanging out with other kids my age after school, I would head over to the hospital, where my dad usually stayed. He had Krohn's disease and seemed to contract every other illness imaginable throughout his life. His health was always so poor. He ended up having over a hundred surgeries in his lifetime. To be with him,

I often went straight to the hospital after school and spent my day there. Dad and I would watch movies, eat at the hospital cafeteria together, or just talk. I loved football and had a goal to play in college, so Dad often talked with me about football.

Making it to my athletic events in junior high and high school was tough for my dad because he was so sick. Still, there were only a few he missed. He found a way to come and watch me. I felt like I needed him there. Because he was my best friend, I felt that if he watched me, I could play with extra confidence. I performed better when he watched me. He knew that, and even when in the hospital, he would find ways to be there for me.

I remember this one wrestling match I was losing. I was struggling to keep my opponent from turning me over and pinning me; he had almost beaten me. While I struggled not to get pinned, the double doors of my high school gym opened and in walked my dad. He was sweating because of pain, but immediately his eyes met mine and he smiled. He pumped his fist to encourage me. Immediately, that wrestling match changed. I wrestled with extra desire—I was not going to lose while Dad was watching. I ended up winning! My family and friends congratulated me, but they also approached my dad inquisitively, asking, "Aren't you supposed to be at the hospital?"

"It's the darndest thing," Dad explained. "The nurse in my hall—she knows how much I wanted to see Brock wrestle, so she gave me special permission, just for one hour, to come and watch." My friends and relatives congratulated him with hugs, saying, "That's so nice of her. We're so glad you're here!"

Overhearing this, I chuckled to myself. I knew the strict rules at the hospital and that they would never in a million years let my dad leave the hospital unattended. I got real close to him and said under my breath, "They didn't really let you leave, did they?"

Dad wiped the sweat from his brow and looked left and right, making sure everybody was out of earshot. "Don't tell anybody," he replied. "I've gotta get back. I'm gonna be in so much trouble."

By the book, what my dad did wasn't a good decision. He was an honest person, but he did anything he could to support me, and that meant everything to me. My dad wasn't perfect, but how he loved me! He really, deeply loved. He taught my siblings and me many lessons throughout our lives, but honestly, the greatest thing he ever taught was the lesson he didn't teach with words. He loved us so much, and he sacrificed so much to be there for his kids. He taught us love without saying a word.

My grandparents recently told me a story I never heard. A neighbor of theirs once told them something he had seen after one of my high school football games. He had been selling concessions during the game, and after the game ended he closed up and headed back to his car. He was surprised to see another car in the parking lot; usually, it was all vacated by the time he finished.

He got into his own car, turned on his headlights and looked around for the owner of the other car. He saw two shadows moving slowly in the light. As they came closer, he saw my little brother, Jared, trying to hold Dad up, with Dad leaning on him. They were slowly making their way to our car, but Dad, wincing in pain every few steps, would fall onto Jared, who would do his best to hold onto Dad so he wouldn't fall. Dad had used every ounce of energy he had to watch my game. He fought through pain and fatigue to watch me, and when it was over, he didn't have enough strength to make it back to the car. Neither Dad nor Jared ever told me; I never knew the pain Dad went through that night to support me until I heard that story.

My father's battle against disease and the incessant problems caused by side effects of medications lasted the entire time I knew him. Through those trying times, however, the Lord gave our family many beautiful, tender mercies. While my father was in a coma for two months, several members of my family felt impressions that his spirit was somehow with us and that he was able to watch over us. When my father came out of the coma, he testified that he had seen the spirit world and had indeed come, with deceased family members, to watch over us. He wrote a book and shared his experiences, adding his own personal witness to what prophets have shared since the beginning of this Church—families can be together forever. Having a part of this with him, I can submit my own word that while my dad was a perfectly normal man, his experiences really did happen.

About six months after high school, I received my mission call to Montevideo, Uruguay. My final farewell to Dad was a tough one, but I was filled with the excitement and energy of the Spirit. I was going to the MTC! Listening to General Authorities speak to us every week, continually studying the gospel, and learning a new language provided such a rich and varied experience for me. As excited as I was, however, I really missed my dad. It was ironic, because I was so continually enveloped in the Spirit and full of joy, yet every once in a while I felt as if my heart cried out, "Please, Heavenly Father, please help me feel the strength my dad used to give me."

I happened to be reading in 2 Kings one day in the study room. In the story, Elijah and Elisha were traveling together toward Beth-el, where Elijah would be taken up to heaven in a chariot of fire. Elijah and Elisha refer to each other as *father* and *son*, so the story immediately connected with me. Elijah knew that once he arrived at Beth-el, he'd be taken into heaven and several times asked his "son" to let him go alone. Each time, his "son-prophet" Elisha emphatically replied, "As the Lord liveth, and as thy soul liveth, I will not leave thee" (2 Kings 2:2). As I read, this story began to connect with my own thoughts and feelings more and more. When the two prophets finally arrived at Beth-el together, Elijah turned to Elisha. "Ask what I shall do for thee, before I be taken away from thee." Elisha's reply to his "father-prophet" caught me off guard: "I pray thee, let a double portion of thy spirit be upon me" (2 Kings 2:9).

Suddenly, emotions overwhelmed me. I couldn't hold back the tears. I missed Dad, and I knew what I wanted. I silently prayed the mightiest prayer of my life: "Heavenly Father, please, let a 'double portion' of my dad's spirit be upon me, even if he can't stay with me physically."

I felt a calm assurance that this prayer would be granted. Two days later, the MTC president called me into his office and sat down with me. "Son, I have some very bad news. Your father passed away this morning."

What? My world suddenly turned upside down. I had asked for a double portion of Dad's spirit to be with me—now he was gone? The MTC president spoke again, and his voice interrupted my thoughts, as if in response to them: "I am sure, Elder, that this death was not by coincidence. Your father was meant to go into Uruguay with you and teach the ancestors of the people you teach."

Click. A "double portion" of my father's spirit would "be upon me." It made sense. I was full of so much grief, but for that one moment peace seemed to outweigh the pain. My prayer was answered. Dad was going with me to Uruguay, and together we would teach by the Spirit. We would be companions like Elijah and Elisha, never to be separated again, so long as we could both prove faithful.

I don't know exactly how to connect the dots here. Did my prayer cause this to happen? I don't think so. Did Heavenly Father know my dad would soon pass, and thus He planted in me the desire to pray like I did? I don't know. I only know that He answered my prayer, and in an incredibly dramatic way.

I was granted permission to go home for one day and speak at the funeral. I spoke about the movie *The Lion King*. I talked about a scene when Simba looks into a pond and finds his father's reflection staring back at him. Rafiki the monkey, standing beside Simba, commented, "You see? He lives in you." In this scene, Simba realized that his father lived within him and that he had the potential to grow into that reflection. I told everyone at the funeral that when I returned in two years, I hoped they would see my father's reflection in me. Of course, in the end, I was really striving to engrave Christ's image into my own countenance, for I believed that my father had that himself. I felt the Spirit testify through me, stronger than I had ever felt it before.

In the story I read from 2 Kings, Elisha's desire was granted. Elijah was carried up in a whirlwind into heaven, and when Elisha returned to his people, many commented, "The spirit of Elijah doth rest on Elisha" (2 Kings 2:15). Elijah's prophetic calling was upon Elisha.

I sought for no prophetic calling, but my determination was to be like Elisha in the sense that he lived up to what his "father" had been. In two years, when I would return from Uruguay, I hoped that people would notice in me the same Light of Christ that my father had had.

Down in Uruguay, an intense clash of emotions raged within me: heartache as I missed Dad, worry for my family at home, and exhilaration to know that Dad was right beside me as an angel. I also felt a sense of urgency to do my best, knowing he was watching me. I felt an immense gratitude to God for hearing my prayers, knowing how much I needed Dad to be with me—but honestly, there was another side of me that was somewhat confused and angry at God. Why did He allow my dad to die? Dad had been given so many blessings and was promised that he would live. But all of these emotions channeled into one determination: I must live close to the Holy Spirit, as that's the only way to feel Dad with me.

Though I was far from perfect, the Lord did help the warrior in me to emerge. There were times when I lost sight of that inner warrior, but people like Elder Barkle helped me rekindle that flame. Every time that flame of "warrior-hood" reignited, it was like a powerful energy from the Holy Spirit burst from my heart every time I bore testimony. I could not hold back; I knew that the harder I worked, the closer I would be to the Holy Ghost. The closer I was to the Holy Ghost, the more the Holy Ghost would be able to reassure me that my father was still with me. I gave every ounce of effort I had to preach the gospel. I had to testify, somehow, to *every single person*! They all had families too, and they needed to know that they could be with their families forever, just like I could be with my dad and family forever. They needed to know what I knew.

There were times investigators would comment on how much they wished a certain family member who had passed away would have had the chance to understand the gospel. In those circumstances, I would often say, "I have a father who has passed away. I don't know everything that goes on beyond the grave, but I do know that God is merciful and that He knows your concern for your loved one. Maybe my father is assigned to teach your family in the spirit world." The more I bore testimony, the more my testimony felt engulfed in the flames of the Spirit. So much energy came forth every time I bore it. It became perfectly undeniable. Heavenly Father did bring that warrior within me to the forefront.

I got overzealous at times. I think I bothered some people unnecessarily, when it was neither the place nor the time for a testimony. But I was trying, and I think the Lord saw that and blessed me for it. One night, I was on an overnight bus being transferred to a new city. Most everyone around me was sleeping, but that sense of urgency hit me again: *These people need to know that families can be together forever, no matter what happens in this life!*

I got up and took a few steps toward the man who sat behind me. He was out cold, two little kids snoozing with him in his arms. I tapped him on the shoulder to wake him up and explained, "I'm so sorry to wake you, but I have a message more important than anything else—that you can have those little ones forever. We don't have to talk right now; you can sleep, but my companion and I would love to come to your house another time and talk with you more."

He looked at me, bewildered, and said, "No!"

I did not sense such a flat-out response was coming. The weight of what I had done hit me. I suddenly felt incredibly awkward. "I'm sorry," I muttered as I turned back toward my seat. What had I been thinking? Why would somebody want to talk to me right after I woke him up? As I was turning away, however, the man said something that lifted my spirits again: "Te felicito." I'll always remember those words. They were simple, really—Spanish for "congratulations." I almost thought he was mocking me, but I looked back and saw his sincere face. I was kind of surprised by what he had just said, so I said, "Gracias," not knowing if I even was supposed to thank him for a comment like that.

What did he mean? As I thought about it, I hoped it meant something like, "Congratulations on being so dedicated to your religion." I fell back into my seat and cried. What I had just done was probably over the top—it just wasn't the best way to approach somebody with the gospel. However, I knew Dad was watching, and somehow I knew he was happy.

Football coach Vince Lombardi once said, "I firmly believe that any man's finest hour, the greatest fulfillment of all that he holds dear, is that moment when he has worked his heart out in a good cause and lies exhausted on the field of battle—victorious."

I discovered that there was strength and determination within me I'd never known before. I believe that inner warrior, though imperfect, began to emerge, and it felt awesome. Both during the mission and in the years since, however, I have found that I am not unique in that way. I began to recognize many others who have unleashed the latter-day warrior within themselves as well.

BYU Football

I had played football at Snow College for a semester, previous to leaving on a mission, and I rejoined that team in 2006. I joined BYU's football team a semester later, with two years of football eligibility left.

When I joined BYU's team, a few things caught my eye right from the get-go. I walked through the locker room on my first day and felt a little starstruck, recognizing players I had watched on TV. These were undoubtedly warriors on the field, but I began to see that many of these physical warriors were also spiritual warriors. BYU had a different football program than any others I had been a part of. We opened each team meeting with prayer. Then Coach Mendenhall would read a scripture and share a spiritual thought. The first time this happened, I looked around the room to see how other players would react. It was easy for me to tell which team members had allowed their inner, spiritual warrior to be cultivated. Some players did not pay attention, but there were others with whom I could feel a kindred spirit. I saw fire in their eyes; they watched Coach Mendenhall with locked gazes, knowing that spirituality was the key to fully unlocking their warrior spirits. When I saw their eyes, eyes that craved the spiritual nourishment the coach was offering, I could feel a warrior-like strength emanating from them.

Coach did not just share short scriptural thoughts and quickly move onto football; spiritual thoughts were the overriding theme of each team meeting. The Church history film *Only a Stonecutter*[1] became the framework for every thought Coach would share that year. He encouraged us to fulfill our respective roles on the team with a sense of duty and honor, the way John Rowe Moyle (the main character in the film) did with his role as a stonemason of the Salt Lake Temple.

Before an important game, Coach showed Bruce R. McConkie's last general conference address,[2] encouraging us to play every play like it was our last. Players responded to these thoughts with belief that these spiritual insights could bless them in *every* aspect of their lives. I watched them maintain gospel standards around their peers, and then unleash a zealous energy on the field. They played with incredible intensity. I think they understood that they were representing a Church-sponsored school and never wanted anyone to question their level of effort.

So I ended up being the backup to the starting defensive end Jan Jorgensen, so I was not always a warrior on the field. I still believe, however, that my inner warrior was growing. Some of the greatest honors I have ever received from my teammates and coaches included the Floyd Johnson "Shield of Faith" Service Award and LaVell Edwards "Spirit of the Y" Award, given for spirituality and devotion to the cause we were involved in. I also had the honor of receiving the Ultimate Warrior Award, given for hard work in the weight room and service in the community. I felt I possessed the same warrior spirit that many of my teammates had. We craved spirituality together and a vehicle by which we could express the warriors within us. I had begun to find my inner warrior in the mission field, and I was now on a team with about fifty other young men who had found that same thing within themselves.

My teammates and I chose to unleash the fight within us through football, but there are so many fights—so many worthy causes in which to be "anxiously engaged" (D&C 58:27), and one important fight takes precedence over them all: the fight to overcome the temptations of Satan.

While you will find that this book focuses on the warrior-like example I learned from Coach Mendenhall and ten other players, please understand that this is not a BYU football book, nor is the concept of latter-day warriors restricted to BYU football. It comes from the scriptures. BYU football was just one setting in which I found other warriors around me. Coach Mendenhall, in my mind, is certainly a spiritual warrior. The way he spoke with so much fire and intensity of the Spirit about being a true disciple of Christ reminded me of some of the fiery talks I've heard in general conference. This intensity carries over into the way he coaches football, and I believe that this only shows that "those that keep the commandments of God . . . are blessed in all things, both temporal and spiritual" (Mosiah 2:41).

Does that mean you can only be a warrior if you're somehow associated with BYU football? Of course not. This is why I again want to emphasize that this is not a BYU football book. I found others with warrior-like courage on my mission. I saw many missionaries in Uruguay who truly had a warrior-like zeal in the way they preached, and many of them never had been nor would be athletes. If you look, you will find warriors in your school's choir, in an art club, working at a job, or in any other setting. Warriors are those who realize there is a reason they feel greatness within, and whatever they choose to participate in (sports, music, the arts) is only "a vehicle that lends credibility" (in Coach Mendenhall's words) to the real message, which is that they are sons and daughters of a loving Heavenly Father, that they have been redeemed by Jesus Christ, and that they have a divinely called prophet in these latter days.

I hope that the latter-day warriors concept will be recognized as reaching much further than just the realm of BYU football. Who are the spiritual warriors in your everyday environment? You, me, all those around us—we were all warriors in the premortal realm. God has planted the seeds of valor in each one of us, so we have the capacity to become warriors. We must make the choice, however, to fully develop that warrior.

Misdirected Warriors

Since football and college, I've worked in Provo as a seminary teacher. Teaching has become my next battle. As docile as seminary teaching sounds, I have found that working with the youth of the Church is every bit as much a fight as missionary work or football.

Indeed, fighting to help the youth of the Church recognize, through the Holy Ghost, the potential they have within themselves has been an even more intense battle than football. I've seen many, many young warriors who were completely ignorant of what's within them. They didn't understand that they are meant to be something special.

Some warriors have aggressive personalities. They have all this fight bottled up within themselves, and they do not know where to channel it. Loud music, brawls, and parties are examples of things that might be appealing to someone with an aggressive personality, so he or she considers trying to fit into that type of environment. I've seen many of the choicest warriors sitting in the back of my seminary classes, eyes void of spiritual conviction. Why? It's not because they were born with less spirituality. In fact, they were born with such great raw potential that it seems as if they cannot figure out how to control or handle it. Ironically, the inner fight some youth find within themselves is only controlled "by long-suffering, by gentleness and meekness, and by love unfeigned" (D&C 121:41). When controlled appropriately, it becomes the fire that gives people the strength to walk away from evil, to speak up when no one else will, and to keep praying and reading the scriptures when others would quit.

The talents and traits within the youth are there for a reason. The fighting spirit inside was never meant for profane music or violence. In the premortal existence, it was used for bold testimony and unyielding faith. It was not meant for rebellion against parents but rather to defy the forces of evil that lurk around us. "For we wrestle not against flesh and blood, but against principalities, against powers, against the rulers of the darkness of this world, against spiritual wickedness in high places" (Ephesians 6:12).

Another kind of warrior I sometimes see sitting in seminary is warriors who don't believe they are warriors. They might be too timid or shy to think there is any degree of fight inside. As you'll read in this book, Bryan Kehl was actually one of those types. Up until eighth grade, he was shy and under-confident, but he had a miracle take place in his life, in which he gained confidence in his own warrior spirit within.

Today, I consider Bryan one of the most confident athletes I've ever met, yet he maintains humility. I have another friend who also felt under-confident before leaving on his mission. He received a priesthood blessing just before leaving; a key line from this blessing stuck with him ever since: "You were a warrior in the premortal life, and it's time for you to step into your strength." My friend took that blessing to heart and attacked missionary work like few young men I've ever known. He even stood up on buses and testified to everyone on them like Elder Barkle did.

But youth today can sometimes think like Bryan used to think. When they hear of the great potential that latter-day youth have, they sometimes say (consciously or subconsciously) to themselves, *Surely, I'm not the one with that much potential.* They are good and righteous, but they don't believe in the great things they can become. I anxiously yearn inside for them to discover what Bryan and others like him discovered within themselves.

A third group of students and warriors I have observed are those who have great potential inside and yet they reject it. These students believe they *could* be great and sometimes tell themselves that they will be—someday. But for now, they are distracted and procrastinate away what could have been a focused, hunger-filled journey toward God. Satan produces some video game, addiction, or premature relationship with the opposite sex that sucks the spiritual life and vigor out of them. I believe that the adversary uses this tactic of distraction against some of the greatest warriors because he is terrified of what these powerful youth will become if they make the unyielding decision never to be caught in these traps again.

Warriors in the Scriptures

Is it any secret that Heavenly Father, through the scriptures, attempts to connect with our inner warriors? Countless scripture stories use battle as a metaphor for the fight we wage against Satan.

Captain Moroni's heroic fighting spirit was enough to shake the foundations of hell itself: "If all men had been, and were, and ever would be, like unto Moroni, behold, the very powers of hell would have been shaken forever; yea, the devil would never have power over the hearts of the children of men" (Alma 48:17).

The stripling warriors "fought as if with the strength of God; yea, never were men known to have fought with such miraculous strength; and with such mighty power did they fall upon the Lamanites, that they did frighten them" (Alma 56:56).

Young David's unconquerable spirit shows that warriors come in all sizes. What David, a youthful boy said to a man probably double or even triple his size shows the righteous defiance he had within him:

> Thou comest to me with a sword, and with a spear, and with a shield: but I come to thee in the name of the Lord of hosts, the God of the armies of Israel, whom thou hast defied. This day will the Lord deliver thee into mine hand; and I will smite thee, and take thine head from thee; and I will give the carcases of the host of the Philistines this day unto the fowls of the air, and to the wild beasts of the earth; that all the earth may know that there is a God in Israel. (1 Samuel 17:45–46)

The Apostle Paul, who spoke often of his constant painful affliction, still lived a warrior's life. He fought with no physical weapon, and yet he used a powerful metaphor near the end of his life: "I have fought a good fight, I have finished my course, I have kept the faith" (2

Timothy 4:7). In a letter to his beloved brother in Christ, Timothy, Paul challenged him to do the same: "Fight the good fight of faith" (1 Timothy 6:12). Paul, in word and deed, lived a warrior's life.

Enoch was one of the greatest prophets since Adam. His powerful speeches exemplified that even a man's voice can become his weapon. Indeed, his powerful speaking ability stands before us as a symbol of the weapon we too must use in these latter days; it is imperative that we, today's warriors, speak up. "And so great was the faith of Enoch that he led the people of God, and their enemies came to battle against them; and he spake the word of the Lord, and the earth trembled, and the mountains fled, even according to his command; and the rivers of water were turned out of their course; and the roar of the lions was heard out of the wilderness; and all nations feared greatly, so powerful was the word of Enoch, and so great was the power of the language which God had given him" (Moses 7:13).

The Prophet Joseph Smith was also an amazing warrior in the way he spoke. In November of 1838, he testified against prison guards who held him captive and chained as they bragged of hideous crimes they had committed against Mormons. According to Elder Parley P. Pratt, Joseph "arose to his feet, and spoke in a voice of thunder, or as the roaring lion, uttering . . . 'Silence, ye fiends of the infernal pit. In the name of Jesus Christ I rebuke you, and command you to be still; I will not live another minute and hear such language. Cease such talk, or you or I die this instant.'"

Elder Pratt recorded what happened next: "He stood erect in terrible majesty. Chained, and without a weapon; calm, unruffled and dignified as an angel, he looked upon the quailing guards, whose weapons were lowered or dropped to the ground; whose knees smote together, and who, shrinking into a corner, or crouching at his feet, begged his pardon, and remained quiet till a change of guards" (*The Autobiography of Parley P. Pratt* [Salt Lake City: Deseret Book, March 2000]). Joseph Smith quite possibly became one of the greatest warriors of all time in that moment, and without any weapon other than his own voice.

How This Book Began

Knowing the greatness of scriptural and historical heroes like these, and feeling the importance of the youth of the Church understanding who they can become, I've tried as a seminary teacher to help young men and women see the warrior potential they have within them. I began writing some of my impressions down, hoping one day to compile them into a book.

One morning in the summer of 2012, I woke up with the impression that I should ask Coach Mendenhall for help. I went to his office and explained what I had been working on and my idea of writing a book. I told him about some seminary students I had seen and known and about the warrior-like strength I could see in their eyes, as well as my concern that they did not see it in themselves.

I talked to him about how impressed I had been with the young men I had played with on the team, how they seemed to exemplify that warrior spirit I hoped I could motivate the youth to see within themselves. I asked him who he had considered to be the warriors of our football team, both spiritually and physically. Coach gave me a list of ten names and their contact information so that I might interview them.

Each interview constitutes one chapter in this book. In each succeeding chapter, you will read about a young man who truly unleashed the warrior soul within himself, both physically and spiritually. In many cases, you will also read about these players' beloved wives. These great women generally received none of the recognition that BYU football players typically get, but they are so loved and admired by their husbands. In their own ways, they also became warriors.

As a disclaimer to my fellow teammates, I know many more of you would qualify to be a part of this book. I can think of many mission companions and teammates who exemplified a warrior spirit, as Coach Mendenhall also remarked. Admittedly, when Coach gave me the list of names, he said, "These are just a few names off the top of my head."

However, there was something so special, so inspired that happened in each interview, I have begun to ask myself, "Was it just a coincidence that Coach happened to think of these ten men's names?" Interview after interview, I've been more and more convinced that nothing in the making of this book has been coincidence.

I firmly believe Coach was inspired, because each of these players revealed such a unique story and shared experiences that need to be told in these latter days, when we desperately need examples of what a real warrior is. As you will see when you read each chapter, the players in this book were meant to be in it. Each player, in one way or another, has developed a warrior within himself and can serve as an example to all of us. You can strengthen the warrior within you and join in the final battle against the adversary!

Notes

1. This film can be found online in the media library of the Church's website. Enter *Only a Stonecutter* into the lds.org homepage.

2. See Bruce R. McConkie, "The Purifying Power of Gethsemane," *Ensign*, May 1985.

JOHN BECK

"Doubt not, fear not" (D&C 6:36).

*A*s I started *making calls to the players Coach had mentioned, John Beck was the first to set up a meeting. Everyone I contacted was kind and sincere, but many explained they would need to talk with their wives and plan a time for me to come. John answered the phone and scheduled with me immediately. "Can we do it tomorrow?" he asked. I was caught a little off guard by his readiness. "You caught me at a perfect time," he said. "I'm headed to Houston's training camp on Monday, and my wife and kids are already down there getting our apartment ready, but I'll be in Provo this weekend. Max Hall and I have a little tradition—right before we head into training camp, we play a round of golf with the bishop of our old student ward. How about you come over to my house a few hours before we go golfing?"*

I was surprised—he did not know who I was (I joined the team in 2007, and his senior year was 2006), and he was heading into an intense NFL training camp in just a few days. But he was immediately willing to meet with me. I expressed some of my surprise to him. He responded, "Hey, it sounds like you're doing a great thing— I'd love to be a part of it!"

The next day, he came out of his apartment building to meet me and led me up into his home. He talked with me on the elevator as if we had been friends for years. I wondered if he was this open and friendly with everyone. We entered the apartment, sat in the front room, and began to talk.

As we talked, he explained he had decided at an early age he was going to play in the NFL. When he was a kid, he would tell people about his dream, and some ridiculed him. He initially felt anger, but what made him great in my opinion was that he allowed the Lord to replace the anger with something more positive, constructive, and edifying. John learned to control his anger and channel it into determination. In his determination to overcome disbelief from others, he grew spiritually and physically. Spirituality helped John to correctly channel, not stifle, his inner drive. Apparently, his aggressive side was evident even in early childhood.

John: "When I was a little kid, I got in tons of fights. I was in the principal's office at the elementary school all the time. I had good parents—they just said, 'You know what? We have a kid who has a little fire to him.' They helped me see that there was a purpose to all of that. It was still hard to channel, and it was a struggle I had for years. I remember one time in high school, I was straight-up ready to fight a kid. He knew about my football dreams and told me, 'You're never gonna make it. You have no chance,' and I said, 'I'm ready to fight you right now!' It was on our way to seminary."

As John talked about the aggression he felt during his childhood and adolescence, I had the impression that courage and determination were perhaps some of John's greatest strengths in the premortal existence and were simply misinterpreted as feelings of aggression during John's early mortal life. John later learned what his fighting spirit was originally meant for. He admired and resonated with one of the greatest examples we have of courage and determination: Captain Moroni.

John: "I think of Captain Moroni—where the scriptures say that if every man were like Moroni, 'the devil would never have power over the hearts of the children of men' [Alma 48:17]. Moroni had a warrior spirit in him, and I felt like I did too. There's no way I would have played football if I didn't have that. If a kid has some fight in him, I see it as a blessing if it's cultivated in the right way. I think fiery people are sometimes the most passionate people. They have opportunities for greatness because of the drive within them. They only have to get that drive pointed in the right direction.

"It's like the Liahona. I like to think we all have a kind of Liahona inside ourselves. Our talents, skills, and desires all drive us in a certain direction. Well, what direction is that? If you aren't living your life the way Heavenly Father wants you to, you're pointing that Liahona yourself. You're just going in your own direction. But when you're doing the things Heavenly Father wants you to do, He can help channel your inner drives and get them pointed in the right direction. Then there's a purpose. You have to understand who you are in God's eyes. You must understand where you came from and where He wants you to end up.

"I learned that was all I had to do. During those early years, everybody saw this little red-haired, freckle-faced kid when they looked at me, and thought, *He's not going to achieve all these dreams he has.* I just had to channel my inner drive into accomplishing my dreams rather than getting mad at them. I was small as a kid because I matured so late, but I always told people, 'I'm going to be a quarterback in the NFL.' I had this mentality like I was the underdog, and that's what started all the hard work. I wasn't going to let anybody make my ship swerve; I knew where I was going. I wasn't afraid of how other people would view me. When I heard people say, 'You're not going to make it,' I learned to channel all that into determination. People would hear about my goals, or what I did, and say, 'Who does this guy think he is?' But they didn't know me. I thought, *You don't know how much drive I have. You don't know how much this means to me.*

"I remember my football coach told me one day, 'Listen, you're never going to be a quarterback. You have a good arm, but you're too small.' He made me play receiver and defensive back. I remember thinking, *This coach doesn't know me five years from now. He doesn't know I'm going to grow.* I played on a Pop Warner team too that year, and I was the quarterback for that team. There were certain things I believed in. I just had to have thick skin toward anybody who didn't believe."

Captain Moroni also dealt with doubters who didn't believe in the cause he was fighting for. This is perhaps one of the reasons John resonated so much with him. The king-men (Alma 51:5), as they were called, didn't believe in Moroni's fight for freedom. But Moroni knew that courage and belief are contagious, and that as long as he was valiant, those who had desires for freedom would follow him. Moroni wrote, "And except ye . . . come out and show unto me a true spirit of freedom. . . . I will come unto you, and if there be any among you that has a desire for freedom, yea, if there be even a spark of freedom remaining, behold I will stir up insurrections among you" (Alma 60:25, 27). Moroni knew that belief in his cause would catch fire, and it did: "He did raise the standard of liberty in whatsoever place he did enter, and gained whatsoever force he could. . . . And it came to pass that thousands did flock unto his standard, and did take up their swords in the defence of their freedom" (Alma 62:4–5).

Even when the setting isn't war, anyone's unyielding belief in a cause can become contagious. Warrior spirits have within them an ability to lead, for evil or for good. People are attracted to courageous belief. Like Moroni, John's belief in what he could do was contagious.

John: "The people who want to climb upward with you will come. They'll follow you. I would call the other kids in my neighborhood block, and I'd draw up workout programs in our backyard. I'd tell them, 'If you wanna be good, you gotta do this workout.' It was what I loved doing. We would prepare for street pickup games too. I would bring them into my house and put on a highlight video to pump them up. I would say, 'If we're going to play this game, we're going to win, so we better get pumped!' Even when outsiders made fun of me, my friends who worked out with me believed. That fight in me kept me going, and I ended up having a successful high school career."

John was named the Outstanding Male Scholar Athlete of Mountain View High School in Arizona. He was the first-team all-region and first-team all-state quarterback as well. In addition, his region named him the Offensive Player of the Year, and Arizona gave him first-team Super All-State and Super All-State player of the year honors. USA Today named him an honorable mention All-American, and Dairy America named him a first-team All-American. He was the

Arizona High School Football Player of the Year and received the Ed Dougherty and Fred Enke Awards, given to the Arizona quarterback of the year. Even Fox Sports named him the Arizona 5A Player of the Year. His team had a 25–2 win-loss record through his junior and senior years, and they won a state championship together to cap off his senior year. John was named the MVP of the state championship game. He later got to play in the Arizona All-Star game and was the MVP of that game as well. He still holds the record for touchdowns in a single season for Arizona high schools: forty-two. He definitely proved the doubters wrong.

John: "I feel like Heavenly Father knew that I had an inner fighter. There's no way I would have been a high school quarterback if I didn't have that. There's definitely no way BYU would have happened later on if I didn't have that. Somebody else would have been quarterback. I think Heavenly Father gave me a fighting spirit, and then trusted me to channel it into the right things. I was given the responsibility to press it into something great."

As glamorous as high school football was for John, learning to channel his inner drive was a preparation for something more important than football.

John: "I can remember my high school coach telling me, 'You don't need to go on a mission. Your Church already has tons of missionaries. Don't go on a mission; just play football.' But I had already learned not to fear people who told me, 'Don't do that.' I'd already gained an attitude of, 'Okay, this is a challenge!' At that point in BYU's history, there had been no quarterback ever to serve a mission, come back, and lead them to a conference championship. No quarterback had ever gone to the NFL and started a game as a returned missionary. So everybody said it's impossible—that I couldn't take that much time off as a quarterback and expect to do it. I believe the fighter within me helped me to respond, 'Well, I'm going to be the first.' So I left on my mission to Lisbon, Portugal.

"In the beginning, I went on my mission thinking, *I'm a good kid.* I didn't drink. I didn't party. I held callings in my ward. I went to church every Sunday. Some of my peers were drinking and smoking weed—stuff like that. I wasn't doing any of that. I felt like I was a good kid. What I hadn't realized was that I needed to let the Lord shape me. I had always had a strong testimony, but before the mission, I felt uncomfortable sitting down and talking about the scriptures or the way the Spirit feels. I did love scripture stories, but I felt uncomfortable talking about them. On the mission, I learned not to be ashamed to say, 'I love this scripture' or, 'This scripture makes me feel this way.' I just opened up and let the Lord mold me into who He wanted me to be, because who He wanted me to be was the best I could be."

In Abraham 2:8–9, the Lord told Abraham, "I know the end from the beginning; therefore my hand shall be over thee. And I will make of thee a great nation, and I will bless thee above measure, and make thy name great among all nations."

John learned for himself that the Lord would make more of his life than he could on his own.

John: "If only I worked on me, I could get to this point. [Held his hand out, indicating a level a little below his chin.] But, if I let the Lord work on me, I could get to this point. [Indicated a level far above his head.] When I really learned who the scriptural heroes were, I learned what Heavenly Father wanted me to be. Up until that point, I was just trying to be a good kid making good decisions. I avoided a lot of bad things, but there's a difference between avoiding bad things and learning, from the scriptures, the type of person Heavenly Father wants you to be. That's when you realize your potential. That's when you realize your path. You realize it's hard; you realize it's upward. I always knew the stories of Nephi, Moroni, and Helaman, but did I really know the people? When you really learn who the people are, all of a sudden, you see the attributes in them and say, 'I need that. I can get myself there too.'

"That was the first thing I told my brother when I got home. 'Don't worry about geekiness or feeling weird talking about the Church. No, those things are the most important things, and that's how you say, This is who I am.' Football players aren't usually the ones who stand up in seminary, bearing their testimonies with tears in their eyes. Well, that's who Heavenly Father wants us to be. He'll still let us be football players, and He'll use us in different ways, but we have to take that chance and bear testimony. Take that chance, and you know what? You could become a leader for good."

After his mission, John came to BYU on a football scholarship. He dove back into the trying to accomplish his football dreams, but John would soon find a girl worth more to him than even football: Barbara Burke.

John: "We met at a UVSC dance. She had just transferred from Snow College. When I met her, I had actually been praying, asking God to only give me feelings to pursue a girl if she was going to be someone important. I was heading into my freshman football season, and I wanted to be totally focused with no distractions. I had decided I would only hang out with friends one night of the weekend, not both. I wanted to use the other night to study our offense and prepare myself as best I could, heading into my first fall camp since high school. (I had missed three football seasons.)

"One night as I was studying, some really good friends from my mission called me. They were in town and wanted me to go to the UVSC dance with them. At first, I wanted to tell them I had to stay and study, but I felt it was something that would be really fun with some guys I hadn't seen in a while, so I went. If it had been anyone besides guys from my mission, I probably wouldn't have gone. I can remember walking around the dance, seeing tons of pretty girls, but remembering my prayers to only have feelings for someone if she was going to be important.

"At the dance I saw a tall, beautiful blonde I couldn't take my eyes off. I wanted so badly to get her number, but I kept reminding myself of my prayers. I thought, *If she really is someone important, Heavenly Father will help us cross paths again.* When I left the dance that night and was getting into my car, a feeling came over me that she was someone important and I needed to find her again. I told the guys in my car we would need to look for 'that tall blonde I pointed out earlier.' I backed out of the parking spot, rolled the windows down, and said, 'Okay, guys, time to find her!' I had barely finished my sentence when my friend's arm came pointing from the back seat. 'You mean her?' he asked. She just happened to be walking with her friends right toward my car. What were the odds that, in a parking lot full of cars, she happened to be walking right toward my car in the moment I decided to look for her? I pulled up next to her, got her number, and the rest is history.

"We just hung out as friends the first few weeks of my freshman season, and then we started dating seriously near the end of that season. Though we were friends in the beginning, she called and left a message that I will always remember after the first BYU game I ever played in. I had thrown an interception on my first collegiate pass. I was really frustrated on the way home. When I got to my house, I saw my phone had a voice message. It was her, leaving words of encouragement. I barely knew her, but it was my first glimpse into the type of person she is. She's been supporting me every step of the journey since. We dated for ten months and were married in the Manti Temple on May 1, 2004."

Barbara gave John the loving support he needed in a rocky beginning to his football career. John had joined the team at a critical point in BYU's history. The Cougars almost always have winning seasons, but in John's first year, BYU had four wins and eight losses. John would be pushed into a leadership position right away, and he felt the weight of responsibility to restore BYU's winning tradition.

John: "I had to have thick skin. The program was struggling, and all fingers wanted to point at the quarterback—the quarterback and the head coach. My freshman year, I had just arrived home from the mission and hadn't played any college football before, but the third game of the season, the starter broke his hand, and all of a sudden I was the starter! That was when I threw that interception and Barbara called to encourage me. I needed her encouragement, because I hadn't played football in three years. I had to go through all of my learning experiences in the stadium, on TV, in front of everybody, so I really had to have thick skin.

"We got married, and Barbara's support was a lifesaver because my sophomore season was really tough. I had games when I struggled, games that were so frustrating. I had to maintain that same attitude from before: 'If I keep working, this is where I can get to. I have to keep climbing upward.' I just held onto that attitude. BYU was in a mess, and people were pointing at me, like, 'This guy stinks.' I just stuck with it; I just said, 'I'm going to keep fighting.'

"It was really hard. I could tell you about nights when I couldn't sleep—two in the morning, and Barbara and I were just standing there in our kitchen. I couldn't believe the situation I was in. I was trying so hard, working as hard as I could, bringing film home and watching it, talking to everybody and trying to motivate the team, but we were still struggling. I felt like it was on my shoulders to bring us back to dominance."

John ended up with another disappointing five wins to six losses that year. Coach Mendenhall was appointed as the new head coach at the end of the season. John's junior season in 2005 started with a 3–20 loss to Boston College, and Coach Mendenhall was booed off the field. Mendenhall also underwent intense scrutiny, both for taking the helm while the team was struggling and for his attempts to involve spirituality as a central focus for the team. However, many players, including John, believed in his spiritual approach.

John: "If you talk to all the people [in this book], they're going to say, 'I feel lucky because my football coach would stand in front of me and talk about scriptures.'"

The Cougars' record improved slightly that year, with six wins and six losses. They were invited to a bowl game for the first time since 2001. John's success as an individual player also started. He earned first-team all-conference honors and was named the team's offensive MVP. Against TCU that year, John threw for 517 yards and 5 touchdowns. With hard work and patience, John's brilliance was again beginning to emerge. Still, he would not allow himself to get too comfortable.

John: "Once again, the fighter, the passionate side in me was what kept me going. There was never a day when I felt like, 'I'm good enough now. If I can just keep going strong, I'll be fine.' I felt like my whole life had been a climb upward. As a kid, it was a climb upward. On my mission, it was a climb upward. So at BYU, even after things got better, I wasn't going to quit climbing upward. And when you're always trying to go upward and forward, people around you notice, and they want to work with you. I've never had a problem calling guys and saying, 'Hey, you wanna come catch? You wanna put in some extra work?' There were those who were more than willing to do it. Some of my greatest friendships started that way; Nate Meikle caught so many passes with me in the off-season. We have such a good friendship now because we worked our tails off before and after practices."

"For after much tribulation come
the blessings" (D&C 58:4).

When he was a senior, ESPN ranked him as the second-best quarterback in the country. The team's unity was also at a high—the Cougars had an overall season record of eleven wins and two losses and had undefeated conference- and home-game records. John was a finalist for the Davey O'Brien and Unitas Golden Arm Awards. There was also talk about him being nominated for the Heisman Trophy. He was named the Walter Camp Football Foundation National Offensive Player of the Week after his unforgettable last-second comeback against the University of Utah.

John: "My biggest play against Utah—throwing that last-second touchdown—nobody knows everything I had to push through to get there. If I didn't overcome the other trials while I was at BYU, that play might never have happened. My greatest play as a BYU player came after years of pushing through hard times.

"I always think about that Utah game. Without the things I went through at BYU, there's no way that moment would've happened. There were years of tough times that made it possible. I had to keep picking up and moving forward.

"And it wasn't just one play. People forget that we had a fourth down at midfield at another point in the game. Their whole stadium was jumping up and down. The whole thing was gonna be over on that play. Luckily, we were able to convert on that down, but if we hadn't, the opportunity for a winning touchdown never would have happened.

There were so many plays that went into it. Then, at the very end, there was one culminating moment.

"I stood there, looking at the scoreboard. It said we had, like, 3.2 seconds left. It was the most calming feeling I have ever felt; I can't even explain it—just standing there, getting ready. I had wanted that moment so bad, wanted to be in that situation for so long because of all the other times that it hadn't turned out right. I had worked so hard, thinking, *When I get in that moment of the most clutch, I want to be ready.* And all of a sudden, that moment was there."

John received the snap in the shotgun position and scanned the field for open receivers, but he found none. The offensive line was holding strong, and John found himself unhurried by rushers, so he continued to scan the field. The official game clock expired. Utah's defense covered each receiver like glue. Six seconds passed, and still nobody was open.

After about seven seconds, Utah defender Joe Jiannoni broke into the backfield and bolted toward John, in the hopes for a sack. John scrambled right, barely evading him, but Jiannoni continued in pursuit. Right then, Cougar receiver Johnny Harline broke open in the end zone. Being chased to the right, John jumped into the air and threw across his body to the left. Harline fell onto his knees and made the catch. BYU beat rival Utah for the first time in five years! (YouTube "John Beck to Johnny Harline" for a recap of that play.)

John and the Cougars went on to finish his senior year with a 38–8 Las Vegas Bowl victory against Oregon. It was the first bowl victory BYU had in ten years. The program was beginning to rise. John threw for 375 yards and two touchdowns and ran for another touchdown, ending that season as the Mountain West Conference Offensive Player of the Year and a Sporting News second-team All-American. There was just one milestone left in order to accomplish the dreams he'd had as a boy: becoming a starter in the NFL. With this goal, however, also came a spiritual challenge: Could he keep his standards in a culture where morals were often so low?

John: "So now I play in the NFL, and I'm a nerd to everyone else. I'm this Mormon kid who doesn't party or swear—on the football field, I say, 'Freak!' I take time out of the week to go to the temple. I bring my journal to games. No big tough dude writes in journals. I listen to the

BYU Men's Choir on Sunday mornings while I shower and get ready for games. I do a little sacrament meeting in my room [approved of by John's bishop]. That's geeky. That's nerdy to everyone else.

"One time, another player came and told me, 'If you dropped the F-bomb, we would all follow you more.' I said, 'Even if you would follow me more, I'm not doing it.' I didn't really care what that guy thought. I was doing the things I knew affected my life in the right way. Who was that guy? I knew the game. A player can think he's going to be some big stud by saying those words, but he's also going to be some kid's dad. He's going to be some girl's husband. By saying those words, will he be the man that girl always wanted to marry? Will he be the man his son wants for a dad? You have to take the risk of allowing spirituality into your life. I'm not afraid of reading the scriptures or being so full of the Spirit that my eyes tear up. Those are good things. When you raise a kid, you can't be the fiery football player all of the time. Sometimes, you have to be that tender father who can put his arms around his son and tell him he's loved.

"Now, does that mean you can't be a fiery football player? Heck no! Ammon went and chopped a bunch of dudes' arms off. David slung a stone and killed a giant. Look at Moroni or Helaman. You'd have to be a bit of a stud if you're going to lead two thousand people into war. These guys weren't just marching down the road in a parade—they were going to war.

"So there are certain people who are destined to have a little fight to them. And as a leader on a football team, you have to be fiery. I would always get fired up in games. That side has helped me. When I'm on the practice field, I'm working my tail off; I'm intense. At the same time, I know there's a line I will not cross, and I don't need to cross it. If they really look to me as a team captain, I don't have to use swear words to get them in the huddle. As a leader, people will be drawn to my hard work, not to dirty language."

President N. Eldon Tanner said, "Every one of us has been foreordained for some work. . . . Always remember that people are looking to you for leadership and you are influencing the lives of individuals either for good or for bad" ("For They Loved the Praise of Men More Than the Praise of God," *Ensign*, November 1975).

John: "Because I'm willing to keep my standards, there are some players who notice and respect me. There are really good guys. Some good Bible-study guys once asked, 'Why do you always come down and get a piece of bread on Sunday mornings?' I was able to tell them about the sacrament, so I've had missionary opportunities like that one. They've never gone the way I'd like, but I keep working at it. In a blessing, I was told I would bring people into the gospel, so I've always felt like I needed to be a member missionary with the teams I'm on. I've been able to give a Book of Mormon to some of my closer friends."

With his standards and his member missionary efforts as his priorities, John has still longed to accomplish his childhood dream of being a great professional football player. While glimpses of greatness have come, he still continues that fight.

John: "When I first made the NFL, the team that I went to was considered the worst team in the league. The coaches got fired, and being a second-round draft pick meant nothing. I had to start from the bottom and work my way back up. I went to the Redskins and finally got to be a starter, but half my team was injured. We struggled, we didn't score points, and I got benched. But I just kept believing and fighting. I feel like Heavenly Father knew about the trials I would encounter and that I would need a little fight in me to overcome them. There's probably no way I'd still be getting opportunities to play on teams if I didn't have that.

"I watch other quarterbacks. I know I'm as talented as they are, and yet they seem to have all the success. Does Heavenly Father care about my football? I don't know. I know He loves me. In the things that are important to me, He wants me to be successful. I work my tail off at it; He knows that. Does Heavenly Father care about my stats? No. But does He care that I love football and that I work for it? Yes. I firmly believe that.

"Sometimes I feel like I would've given anything for the Redskins to work out. Barbara was in love with the area; I loved Coach Shanna-han. I thought my dream was coming into place—I really did—but it didn't, and it knocked me down. When I was released, it devastated my wife and me. But we have had some of the most spiritual experiences as a couple because of that. You can only learn those sorts of lessons when you go through the hard stuff.

"The man who sealed me in the temple to my wife—his dad died on his mission. He called me and told me his story when I was going through this. He told me it was the most devastating thing that had ever happened to him; it about killed him. He thought, *How in the world am I supposed to deal with this, Heavenly Father? I'm trying to serve You on my mission, and You take my father away?* He said they were really close.

"Well, years later, he served as a mission president and had three missionaries lose their dads while on their missions. He told me, 'There is no way I would have been able to sit in that room as their mission president and console them had I not been through it myself.' As he told me his story, I began to understand why he had felt prompted to share it. I was going through some difficult things as well, but I had to believe that it would prove useful later in life.

"After having that talk with my sealer, my stake president in Virginia called me out of the blue: 'I want to come to your house. I have a feeling I need to talk to you.' I had never met the guy, but he was a stake president. (If a stake president says he's coming to talk to you, you open the door.) So he came in, sat down, and said, 'I know you don't know me. I don't know you, but I felt impressed to come over here.'

"He started retelling scripture stories. He talked about Ammon and Nephi and all of the things they had to go through. He explained how Heavenly Father used them, molded them into who He wanted them to be, and then He was able to use them in other aspects than what they had expected. I could feel that those stories connected to what I was going through.

"Neither the stake president nor the sealer had any idea that my wife and I had been fasting. They had no idea we had been praying a ton. We were just praying and fasting for answers, and we got those phone calls and had those conversations.

"As the stake president talked to us, I felt this comforting feeling, like, 'Heavenly Father is there. You didn't have this devastating moment without Him. He was right here, knowing that this was happening and that you would grow from it. Maybe you didn't get what you thought you would out of it, but you got what He needed you to get. Even though you didn't like it, this experience is going to come in handy for something else to come.'

"We have to acknowledge that Heavenly Father sees our trials, allows us to go through them, and helps us get back up. When we experience trials, He's not saying, 'All right, knock him down again,' but He does allow that trial. He's saying, 'You will learn much from this.' We get knocked down, and then He puts His hand out and says, 'Let's get up.' We become something better. We grow closer to the Savior. I can't imagine moving forward in life not having learned what I did from my hardest trials."

In follow-up conversations over the phone since our interview, I've found that John is now playing in the Canadian Football League with the British Columbia Lions. I was excited to hear it, knowing that other great quarterbacks such as Doug Flutie, Warren Moon, and Joe Theismann also started their careers in the CFL and became great in the NFL. I expressed that thought to John, and he responded, "I'm just happy to play some football, wherever it is." He and Barbara have three sons—Ty, Preston, and Grady.

Markell Staffieri

"Learn of me; for I am meek and lowly in heart" (Matthew 11:29).

*A*s I made *calls and set up appointments, I discovered that two of these players lived only forty-five minutes away from each other in San Diego. They had both been some of my favorite teammates—Markell Staffieri and Matt Allen. On a weekend they were available, I drove down with my wife, Stephanie, and daughter, Kinlee.*

We headed to Markell's house first. Markell had played as a middle linebacker on defense with me. I remembered Markell's sense of humor and his fervor for the game being contagious. He made football so much more enjoyable because he played with passion and still loved to laugh. I remember our game against Tulsa in 2007, driving into our opponent's stadium on the bus. Tulsa, Oklahoma, is located in the heart of the Bible Belt, where religion is a passionate issue. Because we belonged to a Church-sponsored school, someone decided to have a little fun with us.

As we drove to the stadium, we found a large banner with a picture of a Tulsa receiver, diving to catch a deep pass. Printed across this picture were the words Joseph Smith can't cover deep. *Though it was only in jest, some of us players began to feel a little anger. Perhaps sensing the tense mood caused by that banner, Markell yelled out, "Joseph Smith can't cover deep? Good thing he isn't a defensive back, then." He eased* the tension and made us laugh. His sense of humor reminded us that we were there to have a good time and play the game we loved.

Experiences like these caused me to really appreciate Markell. He played with intensity and fire, and at the same time he always reminded us to enjoy ourselves. As Stephanie and I drove, I recounted to her some of my favorite memories of Markell.

Markell lived in a nice neighborhood, next to an elementary school. Markell and his wife, Anna (John Beck's little sister), invited us in and introduced us to their two sons, four-year-old Camden and two-year-old Beck. Anna and Markell had met at BYU, and both were athletes. I could tell their sons were little warriors in the making. They were both like their parents: athletic and full of energy.

During the interview, Markell told us about his somewhat rebellious childhood. It was interesting to listen to his stories. He had been like John in the respect that he always had zeal and courage within him, but those feelings were misinterpreted during his youth. The Lord taught Markell meekness to help harness that aggressive side within him. His stories apply to young warriors who have been given more aggressive personalities.

Markell: "Growing up, I was kind of a rambunctious kid, getting in a lot of trouble at school for different things. It was so bad that from sixth grade through ninth grade, I didn't get invited to any of my friends' birthday parties because their parents thought I was an evil influence on their kids! It's funny to look back now, remembering all those moms who feared me. There was a mom that called my grandma and asked, 'Are you related to Markell Staffieri?' She said, 'Yeah, I'm his grandma.' She told my grandma, 'I don't know what his parents are doing, but that kid is trouble.' She went off on my grandma about what a terrible job my parents were doing because I was such a bad kid.

"Then came Halloween in seventh grade. We dressed in all black and toilet papered people's houses, just out creating mischief. We were walking down this little dirt trail. I will never forget the image of that place; it was such a key moment in my life, kind of like how people remember where they were on 9/11, or when JFK was assassinated. This moment forever changed me. All of my friends stopped, and someone started passing around a marijuana joint. I was thinking, *Man, what am I gonna do when it comes to me?* These were the only friends I had known since moving to California when I was eight.

"I was able to turn it down that night, but I didn't know if I could do that time and time again. The rest of that weekend, I remember thinking, *I have to do something about this.*

"I thought of the one kid who could be a good influence on me: Peter Ord. At this point in life, Peter had been in my priesthood quorums at Church, but he was too much of a 'momma's boy' for me. We just didn't mesh. I was too wild for him.

"There was no school on Monday for the holiday, so I'd see my friends again Tuesday during school lunch. Lunch was a big deal in our junior high. Every group—the jocks, the skaters, the preppies—had their place that they ate lunch. The 'cool guys' (I was with them) were up on the hill, underneath this big pine tree. The 'momma's boys,' where Peter was, were down by the food lines. I remember making the decision at lunchtime. I told myself, *I'm not going up to the hill. I'm going to go eat with Peter.*

"Peter's friends always sat in a circle. You had to be part of the group to be able to step into it. I didn't know how all of this was going to go down. I knew my friends would be mad that I didn't go up to the hill. They'd be like, 'What're you doing, dude? You don't think we're cool, or what?' On top of that, I didn't know how Peter's friends were going to accept me. I just tapped Peter on the shoulder and said, 'Hey, do you mind if I hang out with you guys?' He said, 'No problem. Come on.'

"Pretty much from then on, Peter was my best friend. That made all the difference—forming a bond with someone else who understood my values and what was going on. He was like an anchor. We had a lot of similarities. We were both super competitive; we played football and baseball. Having the courage to change the friends I spent all my time with made a major difference in my life. And you know what? It wasn't as hard to change friends as I made it out to be in my head. I think sometimes we get so worked up about how hard change is, but it's really not that hard.

"You are who you surround yourself with. How did I become a leader at BYU? It's because I surrounded myself with greatness. I hung out with John Beck, Cameron Jensen, Kelly Poppinga, Bryan Kehl. If you want to be a leader, hang out with leaders. There's a huge element to surrounding yourself with great people. You will become whoever you hang out with."

"Two are better than one; because they have a good reward for their labour. For if they fall, the one will lift up his fellow: but woe to him that is alone when he falleth; for he hath not another to help him up" (Ecclesiastes 4:9–10). Markell was still friendly with and respectful to his old group of friends. At the same time, he knew that only friends like Peter could "help him up," if he truly wanted to live the gospel of Jesus Christ.

Markell: "In high school, I loved my linebacker coach, Tim Staycer. The spring before my senior football season, he told me he had just gotten married and that he and his wife, Nancy, were expecting their first child. In order to spend more time with his new family, he wasn't going to come back and coach. I told him, 'Well, that's fine with me. Then I'm not playing.' This decision was based on my distaste for the other coaches. I didn't feel that they were good influences on me as a person or as a player.

"He pulled me out of class about a week later and said, 'I've been thinking about what you said. I feel bad that I'm leaving your senior year. I don't want you to quit; I think you can be a great linebacker. I'll make you a deal. If you bust your rear and do everything you can to be the best linebacker there is, I'll come back and coach one more year.' I committed to him that I'd do it. It meant a lot to me that he'd do that for me, which really solidified our bond. Now I wasn't just playing for myself, or my dreams; I was playing to honor our commitment to each other.

"Each year, we had what was called a senior cabinet. The coaches selected a leader from each position to be on the cabinet. They led stretching and running at the beginning of each practice and made important decisions dealing with the team. To be a member of that cabinet was a huge goal for someone like me, who wanted to be the best. I tried to be a good leader throughout the off-season leading up to my senior year. The first day of practice at Torrey Pines [Markell's high school in San Diego], you ran a mile for your conditioning test. Right after that, you sat up in the bleachers, and they announced the senior cabinet. I played running back and linebacker, as well as on some special teams, so I had more than one chance to be on the cabinet.

"They started announcing the leaders for each position. For the linebacker, they picked my friend Jason. I thought, *All right, I can see that.* He was going to be the middle linebacker, calling the plays. They got to quarterbacks and running backs, and they picked our quarterback, David Bradley. I thought, *Well, all right. I guess they'll pick me as the special teams' guy.* But that didn't happen. They picked one of our other running backs, Blake Perry, as the special teams' guy. I remember being so mad, wondering why I hadn't been chosen. I had a temper in high school, and I figured the coaches hadn't picked me because of that, but I knew I was a hard worker and felt like I was a leader.

"Coach Staycer, the coach I loved so much, pulled me aside as we walked up to practice. He said, 'Hey, come here for a second. Are you mad about this?' I said, 'You better believe I'm mad.' He responded, 'I am too. I fought and fought for you. I'll tell you what, prove them wrong. Prove all these coaches wrong. I believe in you; I believe you are the leader of this team. Every practice, every game, show them you're more than what they think you are.'

"So that was my challenge. I worked harder than ever before to prove them wrong. Blake, one of the starting running backs, got hurt halfway through the year, so I became a starter as both linebacker and running back. I worked hard until I could dominate both positions. We had a good year that year, making it to the semi-finals of the CIF championships—California's version of a state championship.

"Each week throughout the season, coaches gave a 'falcon of the week' award to an outstanding player on offense, and another on defense. The 'falcons of the week' were players who showed great performance, sportsmanship, and effort. At the end of the year, all the falcons got together and voted on who the 'falcon of the year' was. The entire team also voted for the MVP of the year. One of my greatest moments was when my teammates voted me as both. There was only one other player in our high school's history to win both of them. That was one of the best feelings I've ever felt. I felt like I had made Coach Staycer proud and proved my critics wrong."

In addition to these team-given awards, Markell was an all-league, all-county, and all-CIF linebacker, amassing literally hundreds of tackles throughout his whole high school career. As a running back, he led San Diego County with an average gain of 9.7 yards gained every time he touched the ball. Not only focused on sports, Markell was also an all-CIF academic athlete his junior and senior years. Recruited by Coach Lavell Edwards and his staff, Markell decided to serve a mission and come back afterward to play for the Cougars.

Markell: "Another big challenge came when I went on my mission. I was called to Brazil. I was excited; my expectations were high. Both my brothers had served missions, so I wanted to honor my family and be an awesome missionary. In terms of worthiness, at first I felt like I was just okay. I knew I hadn't been a perfect kid, but I still felt like I was worthy enough to be on a mission. I went through the MTC, and then was in my area for a month, but my spirit just didn't feel right. I felt like maybe there were things I needed to take care of.

"I called my mission president and said, 'Hey, I need to talk to you; can you come to my area?' We talked, and the decision was made that I needed to return home to take care of things.

"Confessing is hard. It took a lot for me. When I got home, I had to sit down with my stake president. He released me as a missionary and interviewed me. It was humiliating and humbling to sit there and say, 'Maybe I lied to you. And I'm sorry.' I think that's one of the reasons people don't confess. In our last ward, I was a Young Men's president, and I always encouraged the young men to confess if they needed it. I told them, 'Look, the bishop's here to help you. When you don't want to talk to anyone else, please let him help you. He won't hold onto the things you say.'

Access to the bishop is completely open and confidential, and in many cases, it's the only way to truly free a guilty conscience. Christ Himself pleads with those who have sins that burden their consciences: "Will ye not now return unto me, and repent of your sins, and be converted, that I may heal you? . . . Behold, mine arm of mercy is extended towards you, and whosoever will come, him will I receive; and blessed are those who come unto me" (3 Nephi 9:13–14).

Christ gives powerful yet tender metaphors about repentance and confession: "Come now, and let us reason together, saith the Lord: though your sins be as scarlet, they shall be as white as snow; though they be red like crimson, they shall be as wool" (Isaiah 1:18). He also said, "How oft will I gather you as a hen gathereth her chickens under her wings, if ye will repent and return unto me with full purpose of heart" (3 Nephi 10:6). Christ's mercy is endless. He can help you when you need to confess.

Markell: "So many blessings came from one confession. One immediate blessing was the burden that was lifted. I felt free from my sins. Satan no longer had control—nothing to hang over my head. Though coming home was tough, I felt relieved to have a clear conscience.

"So I began moving on in life. I went back to BYU and started playing football again. At first, I felt like my mission was finished. I thought, *Well, that was it. I gave it a shot, but I didn't prepare myself. We'll see where football goes.* Coach Edwards had told me originally, 'Walk on, and after a year, we'll give you a scholarship.' Then Coach Crowton came. He told me, 'I don't know what Coach Edwards saw, but walk on, and we'll see what happens.' So I walked on and had to prove myself.

"I worked my way through fall camp and ended up starting on every special team. I was super excited. BYU had the first game of the season against Tulane for the Black Coaches Association Classic. I was so happy—I called Coach Staycer and my family. I told them all, 'Hey, I'm number forty-two. I'm starting on all the special teams, first game of the season!'

"The Wednesday before the game, I went to the special teams' meeting. Coach Lamb handed out the special teams' books to everybody, showing the starting lineup for each team. I saw in my buddy's book that the rosters were all there, but I wasn't on any of them. Coach Lamb came and told me he didn't have a book for me. I was so mad and embarrassed that, without saying a word, I got up and walked out of the meeting. I went back to my apartment and played some video games to vent.

"I came back a little while before practice, and the trainer, George Curtis, asked me, 'Did Coach Crowton find you? He's been looking for you for the last couple of hours; where've you been?' So Coach Crowton found me a little later and said, 'Where were you? You left the meeting.' I told him, 'Well, apparently I was off all the special teams, so I didn't feel like I had to be there. I left and came back for practice.' Coach said, 'Well, I want to talk to you about that. We think you're better than special teams, so I didn't want to waste a year of your eligibility on that. We want to redshirt you, and you'll play full-time for us after that.' Then he asked, 'What are your plans for your mission? Are you going to finish?'

"I said, 'Right now, I don't really know.' He said, 'I won't tell you what to do, but I will tell you that in my life, not a day goes by that I don't apply a lesson I learned from my mission.'

"It was just a little comment, but it probably shaped the rest of my life. I thought a lot about it. I saw friends of mine, even returned missionary friends, doing the wrong things. I thought, *I don't want to be one of those guys.* I wanted to give everything. Somehow, seeing my returned missionary friends doing bad things deepened my desire to go on a mission. I realized I had no desire to do what they were doing. I wanted to go back out and finish what I had started. When that season ended, I got a new mission call to Columbia, South Carolina.

"I jumped into that mission, gung-ho. This was where I became so grateful I had confessed and become clean. Because I was now ready and worthy, I began to realize how much the Lord truly loved me. I could feel the Spirit back in my life, and the power of the Atonement bolstered me to make better decisions. This time, I was worthy to finish. The amount of growth that took place in my life in those two years couldn't have been done in any other setting. The experiences I had with the people I met and taught on my mission were irreplaceable. The relationships I formed in South Carolina would have never taken place had I not gotten my spiritual life back on track.

"I was forced into some leadership, and I say *forced* because I don't think it was because I was a great missionary. Being a leader taught me so much because I was in a position to help missionaries who had problems. I'll never forget an experience I had with a missionary who came to me for help. He and his companion were having a lot of friction, and he was really struggling. He asked if he could meet with me after a zone meeting. I remember asking him all of the standard questions: 'Are you reading your scriptures? Are you being obedient to the mission rules?' All that stuff. He said, 'Yeah. I'm doing all those things. I don't know what's going on.'

"It's cool how the Spirit works; I've heard people say that the Spirit blesses bishops and helps them forget so they don't hold onto interviews. I think I was blessed in the same way. I don't remember anything I said to him from that point on, but when I was done, he sat back in his chair and started to cry. He said, 'It's not fair.' I asked, 'What's not fair?' He said, 'It's not fair that you have the Spirit strong enough to know that.' Apparently, whatever I talked about was the issue. So we talked it out. It's really cool to know that if you're fulfilling your role and you listen, the Spirit will talk to you. He had a huge problem. I don't know what it was (I don't think it was any grievous sin or anything), but that experience was so cool to me. The Spirit will direct you. You will know how to help people and still respect them so you don't judge them.

"That helped me so much personally because when I had come home earlier from my mission in Brazil, I'd felt a lot like I betrayed the trust of my bishop and stake president. It gave me a different perspective; they don't look at you that way. It kind of helped me move forward.

"For my last transfer, I served as an assistant with Elder Westover. Every day, the mission president would call and say, 'You need to go serve with these missionaries,' or, 'This elder's depressed,' or, 'These elders don't have anyone to teach.' Our whole job was to travel the mission and work in areas that had problems. It was the most fun and the hardest transfer of my mission. I knew that every day I was going into a situation where nothing would seem right.

"In one of the areas, a missionary was discouraged. His name was Elder Pickup—he had been out for about three months. We came to get him excited about the work again, and we went knocking doors. Nobody wanted to talk to us. We literally tracted from the time we left the apartment at 9:30 in the morning to 9:30 at night, when it was time to come home. We didn't get in one door.

"I remember thinking, *I'm supposed to convince this guy that this is good? That this is fun? That this is worth it?* That was another experience where I don't remember what I said. I don't remember talking to him about anything deep or specific. But about three months after getting home, I got a letter from him, and he thanked me for that day. He said that day changed his mission. I can't think of what inspired him. All I remembered was feeling discouraged myself. It was gratifying to know that in some small way, I helped him feel the Spirit. Elder Pickup went on to be a great leader in the mission."

Through meekness and humility, the Lord molded Markell, a rambunctious youth, into a meek, humble, and warrior-like missionary. In Elder Ulisses Soares' October 2013 conference address entitled "Be Meek and Lowly of Heart," he stated, "Upon acknowledging our dedication and perseverance, the Lord will give us that which we are not able to attain due to our imperfections and human weaknesses." Despite Markell's imperfections, he developed meekness, and that indispensable attribute helped complete the warrior within him.

Markell: "So I finished my mission and came back to BYU. Coach Crowton had been impressed during the time I had played under him, so he had also promised me a scholarship for when I came back. Of course, Coach Mendenhall was put in charge while I was gone, and I mentioned Coach Crowton's promise to me in an interview with Coach Mendenhall. He replied, 'I don't know what Coach Crowton promised you, but I won't award a scholarship to anyone on my defense who hasn't proved himself.'

"That made me determined. I worked harder than ever to prove to Coach Mendenhall that I was worthy of the scholarship. Luckily, I caught his eye, and at the end of my first fall camp, I was awarded a scholarship."

During Markell's junior year, he had a serious injury, rupturing all four muscles in his hamstring. One of the four muscles actually detached from the bone and remains rolled up in the back of Markell's leg to this day. This and other injuries became a severe setback to Markell's ability, but he played on.

Markell: "Whether it was my groin, hamstring, or back, I was hurt most of my career at BYU, so I didn't play nearly as well as I wanted to. There was a lot of anger in me because of that. I carried that anger through my senior year, channeling it into hard work. Cameron Jensen was one of my best friends, and we worked so hard together. In the way

I worked, I wanted to say, 'I don't care if I'm injured; I'm the best guy for this job.' I took my injuries as a challenge to do better.

"We had great leaders on the team: Cameron, John, Curtis Brown, Kelly Poppinga, Bryan Kehl, Jan Jorgensen. I tried to follow their examples, and then help inspire others. I felt an affinity to other walk-ons, even after I got a scholarship. I tried to encourage them; I knew what they were going through because I'd come through their ranks.

"One of the highest compliments I've ever been paid was in a press interview with Coach Mendenhall. They talked about the three star linebackers: Kelly Poppinga, Bryan Kehl, and Dave Nixon. Then they asked him where I fit in. He said, 'I like his influence on our team and I like his anonymity. I like leaders who maybe don't seek the spotlight and handle their roles humbly and are just trying to contribute. That is what he does, and that is maybe the highest compliment I can pay.'

"One of my goals was to be the best linebacker to ever play at BYU. I didn't reach that, and it was frustrating, but another goal I had was to leave an impression. To have your coach, who sees you every day, especially Coach Mendenhall—he isn't satisfied by much—recognize that I tried hard and gave the effort was vindicating."

Injuries limited Markell's participation in games, and, as Coach Mendenhall put it, Markell "[didn't] seek the spotlight." However, he was still able to make a significant contribution and accrued some impressive stats. Markell was a starter all four of the years he played at the Y, amassed 132 tackles, had two sacks (including a five-yard sack against Notre Dame), a forced fumble, and two fumble recoveries.

It was during Markell's time at BYU that he met his wife, Anna Beck.

Markell: "Anna and I met at the orientation to be BYU sports and dance camp counselors during the summer. I recognized her in line; I had spoken with her a week or so prior in Legends Grille. I felt awkward not saying anything, so I turned around and said hi, and we started talking. Anna mentioned that she was John Beck's sister, and I waited for the opportune moment—when she went up to the front to gather paperwork—to call John and ask him if I would be able to take her out. He gave his permission and promptly added, 'Can you give her a ride home too? I was supposed to pick her up.' The next night, John, Barb (his future wife), Anna, and I went on a double date to the Nicklecade in Orem. From that night on, I think the only time we didn't go on dates was when I was on a family vacation to Italy.

"Toward the end of summer, we were out on a date, and Anna said, 'You know, I can see myself being married to you.' I responded, 'Well, football training camp starts in three weeks. Can we wait until after the season?'

"We ended up getting married Tuesday, November 28, 2006, in the Provo Utah Temple. It was just three days after the final game of the season—the famous 'Beck to Harline' game against Utah. I couldn't have asked for a better week: Thanksgiving, beating Utah, and then capping it all off with marrying the love of my life."

Anna underwent trials that would prepare her to understand Markell in his. For example, Markell would soon head to the NFL with the Philadelphia Eagles, only to find that his numerous injuries would not hold up in such a setting. Anna was prepared to understand what Markell was going through. She had dreamed of being a Cougarette, a member of BYU's world-renowned dance team and had worked hard her whole life to achieve that goal. She made many sacrifices to make that dream become a reality. However, when she made the team, she found that avenue was not for her. She made the heart-wrenching decision to leave her dream behind. So when Markell's NFL dreams just vanished, Anna provided the spiritual insights necessary to help Markell move on.

Anna: "It was hard, but it really prepared me to meet Markell. He was everything I wanted. I noticed his leadership. When I think of him, I think of a saying: 'Don't marry a man unless you'd be proud to have a son just like him.' I'd feel so proud if our boys turned out just like Markell. I had made a list of things I wanted to look for in a guy. He was all of it. How could I say no? What I experienced with the Cougarettes prepared me to understand what he went through in the NFL too. I always tell him, 'It's too bad that I never got to see you at your best in what you loved and you didn't get to see me at my best in what I loved.' It's nice to have someone understand."

Markell: "Anna's spirituality has really helped me through one of the hardest trials of my life. My hopes for the NFL had essentially ended back in my junior year, with that injury to my hamstring. It effectively ended my chance of any professional football career and really took away any chance I had of accomplishing my goals at BYU. Many times, I've asked myself, *Why did I have to go through this? Why didn't I get better?* I think we've started to find some answers."

Anna: "In my patriarchal blessing, it talks about having an understanding for the trials of my life. If you would have taken me at eighteen and had me pick between dancing or being a wife, it would've been tough. I don't know if I could have given it all up. But now, having these kids, now I know that it's all about them. I told Markell, 'If you hadn't gone through your injuries, if you made the NFL, would you really have been able to leave football?'"

Markell: "Would I have been able to spend as much time with my kids?"

Anna: "Yeah; would you have picked that? Stay close to the Lord because He knows what you're ultimately going to be. He knows where you're ultimately going to find happiness."

1 Nephi 9:6 echoes Anna's sentiments. Nephi reminds us, "But the Lord knoweth all things from the beginning; wherefore, he prepareth a way to accomplish all his works." The Lord knew fatherhood was a greater destiny than football for Markell, though Markell still found ways to channel his fighting, competitive drive.

Markell: "I'm still super competitive. I play city-league softball, and I get really mad in the games. They tell me, 'Dude, relax. It's just for fun.' I'm like, 'Not for me, man.'"

Anna (laughing): "He played co-ed with me at one time, and I could never play with him again."

It was clear that Markell had always dealt with an inner aggression. Stories in the Book of Mormon teach that there's a godlike quality much higher and nobler than aggression: courage. If a young warrior can take the aggression within and channel it into courage, he or she can become like the warriors from the Book of Mormon. Helaman admired and loved the stripling warriors, who fought with great courage. "Never had I seen so great courage," Helaman said of these youth (Alma 56:45). "And they were all young men, and they were exceedingly valiant for courage, and also for strength and activity" (Alma 53:20).

Markell's love for the scriptures continues to help him harness his inner aggression with meekness and channel it into courage. My favorite part of this interview was finding out about Markell's love for the scriptures and how he has used that love to understand and harness the aggressive side within him. He feels a connection with the warriors in the Book of Mormon and pushes the fighter within himself to become like them.

Markell: "Deep inside, we're all fighters—that's what we're talking about, right? We all want to fight against something. But the question isn't, 'What are you fighting against?' The real question is, 'What are you fighting for?' You can expend that fighter energy in great things, or you can just go fight somebody. So many youth focus only on what they're fighting *against*, like strict parents or rules. But you'll never truly accomplish something great until you realize what you're fighting *for*. What is the principle you're fighting for? Is it agency? Is it personal conviction? Once you decide that, you'll be able to avoid a lot of conflict with, say, your parents, because you're now channeling your fighter into a greater purpose."

Anna: "I look at my kids and think that they have some of that. They have fire inside. I watch teenagers in my ward who have a fighting spirit. I think, *You know what? One day, that's either going to be their greatest strength or their greatest weakness. We just have to do all we can to persuade them to be righteous leaders.* It's an awesome characteristic to have. You just have to channel it into the right cause, or else it can become destructive. My oldest has it, and I think to myself, *That kid is going to be a challenge to raise. But if we do all we can to get him fighting for the right things, he can be great.*"

Markell: "Captain Moroni is one of my favorite examples. As a warrior, he was in touch with the Spirit. In some of his earliest battles, the Holy Ghost prompted him to dress everybody in armor. In the first conflict with the Lamanites, the Lamanites ran away because the Nephites were head-to-toe armored and the Lamanites were in loin cloths. They were likely thinking, *How are we going to penetrate that stuff they have on? We've got one little strap of leather. This isn't* *going to work!* Moroni was a great warrior because he was close to the Spirit in his preparation.

"The Lamanites tried another attack later on, led by Zarahemnah. Captain Moroni and the Nephites were dominating. Moroni stopped the fighting and said, 'Zarahemnah, if you give us your weapons and make a covenant that you won't war against us, we'll let you go' [paraphrasing Alma 44:6]. Zarahemnah said, 'Here are our weapons, but I can't make that covenant; I can't tell you what we're going to do down the road' [Alma 44:8]. So Moroni gave Zarahemnah his weapons back and said, 'We will end the conflict' [Alma 44:10].

"I love that because it shows a lot about Moroni. First, it shows the spiritual side. I like the fact that Moroni knew that there's a time and a place to be a fighter. They were dominating the Lamanites; they could have just slaughtered them all, but Moroni was not a murderer. He was not an angry fighter—just a really good fighter. So he stopped, saying, 'Look, you can see that we can kill you at any time. We can wipe you out. That's not the mission here. The mission is to bring peace [Alma 44:1]. Give us your weapons of war, and we'll give you your lives. Just make the promise that you won't come back to war against us.'

"And I love the fact that when Zarahemnah refused, Captain Moroni gave him back his weapons. That shows something. It was like Moroni was saying, 'All right, take your weapons. I won't fight you unarmed. Go get assembled and get your game plan together. We're going to end it.' He even said, 'That ye may become extinct' [Alma 44:7], which I love. That's gotta be the coolest quote! If you ask me right now, that's probably my favorite scripture story.

"And look at Teancum. After battling the Lamanites for a few days, Teancum basically told himself, 'We're doing all right, but honestly, why don't I go in there and kill their king? That'd probably end it.'

"This isn't in scripture, so I don't know how accurate this is. But when I first read this story, I pictured it like this: Teancum called his men into his tent and was like, 'All right, guys, no one's going to know about this, but I've decided we can win this if I go kill their king.'

"According to scripture, he dropped over the wall, put a javelin into the king's heart, went back, and woke everyone up [Alma 51:35–36].

"Again, this part is my interpretation, but he had to have said something like, 'All right, we've got a situation here. I just went up there and killed their king, so when they find out, they're probably going to be pretty mad.' I just have to laugh when I imagine his face: 'Uh, so they're going to be a little mad; I just killed their king!'

"Teancum has a great story. He was a fighter and he dictated what happened in his own life. He didn't aimlessly go through the battles of life. He wasn't the type to say, 'I'm going to fight just to fight.' Teancum was deliberate: 'I can accomplish this task. We're ready for this; we have a great army. We're doing okay, but I'll go finish it right now.'"

Another way Markell channels the energy within him is through service. He's developed an understanding for the statement of the Savior: "Verily I say unto you, Inasmuch as ye have done it unto one of the least of these my brethren, ye have done it unto me" (Matthew 25:40).

Markell: "Usually, people with warrior spirits have a lot of energy. If that energy turns into anger, they might channel it into rebellion. The best way to channel that energy is to go out and serve. I especially love service for those with special needs. My oldest brother has a daughter, Lyla, who'll be in a wheelchair as long as she lives. She's turning five this year, but she may not grow much. She isn't able to do most natural functions; she can't swallow; she can't talk.

"People say special spirits were sent here without the accountability the rest of us have. They don't need to be tried; Satan can't get to them. I don't know what it is, but she definitely brings the Spirit into every room she enters. I don't know how you could possibly work with disabled kids and not feel that.

"Channeling aggressive energy into service can be life changing. Some kids are afraid to be seen around handicapped kids at school. They hold themselves back because if they hang out with handicapped kids, other kids might make fun of them for it. You'll always get pressure to back down from the great things, but you can't hold back. If you want to be a great fighter, a great warrior, you have to have a great cause to fight for."

> ELDER ULISSES SOARES: "[MEEKNESS] IS MOST IMPORTANT WITHIN OUR HOMES AND WITHIN OUR RELATIONSHIPS WITH OUR ETERNAL COMPANIONS. DURING THE 31 YEARS I'VE BEEN MARRIED TO MY SWEETHEART, SHE HAS OFTEN GIVEN ME GENTLE REMINDERS OF THIS AS WE HAVE FACED LIFE'S UNSETTLING CHALLENGES" ("BE MEEK AND LOWLY OF HEART").

Through meekness, Markell has become a great husband to Anna and a great father to his sons. He has been able to teach them to channel aggression into positive energy.

Markell: "That's another reason why I'm so happy I finished my mission right. I look at where I am now as a husband and a father. I'm sealed to my family in the temple. I'm worthy to bless my wife and children when they need a priesthood blessing. None of this would be possible if I had stayed on the course I was originally on.

"In church on Sunday, we were studying Deuteronomy, specifically Moses's farewell speech to his people before he was taken from the earth [Deuteronomy 31–33]. The teacher asked, 'What would your farewell speech to your family include?' As I thought about that, I felt that the most important lesson I can teach my children is love. I hope I can teach them how much my wife and I love them and how much Heavenly Father and Jesus love them. I want to teach them to love others through the words they speak and the service they give. We are all children of God, and every one of us deserves to love and be loved. That's the most important thing that I can show and teach my kids.

Markell now works in the financial industry as a coach and advisor to help people develop strategic financial disciplines to help them reach their goals. In his spare time, he fuels his competitive spirit with road and mountain bicycle races. To fuel his inner spirit, Markell donates a lot of his time to helping the "Thursday's Heroes" program at BYU and the Holly & Bronco Mendenhall Foundation, teaching classes to troubled teens in his community and various other service projects.

Since Markell's interview, he and his family moved to Mesa, Arizona, where they are now raising three children: Camden, Beck, and their new daughter, Sicily (named for Markell's Italian heritage). As a family, they love two things: being outdoors and watching movies. You might often find their family riding bikes, going on hikes, camping, or playing at the beach. Then at night when they're all worn out, you better believe that they'll be huddled up on the couch with some popcorn, watching a movie together.

Matt Allen

"I will raise up unto my people a man,
who shall lead them" (D&C 103:16).

After Markell's interview, Stephanie and I drove the forty-five minutes from Markell's house to Matt Allen's. Traveling along the California shoreline was a beautiful experience. We loved the jagged ridges of rock that were lined with palm trees, the fresh sea air, and the smell of orange groves.

I told Stephanie some of my old memories of Matt as we drove. I remembered Matt having a countenance that expressed testimony; he had a face of purity and worthiness. It was awesome for me to watch someone who probably would have been considered a "Peter Priesthood" outside of BYU be so intense and successful on the football field. Matt was one of our most successful wide receivers and a team captain.

Before we played against Arizona for our home opener in 2007, Matt addressed us for the pre-game speech. Matt had broken his hand and decided to play through the pain, wrapping his hand in foam. His speech revealed both his intense and his sensitive spiritual sides. He shed tears and yet spoke with power and determination as he told us he would go through anything for us, his teammates. He challenged us to be united in brotherly love and to give every ounce of effort for each other. I specifically remember two things: the power with which he spoke, through tears, and the broken hand, wrapped in bulging foam and which he shook as he expressed his determination to us.

In the game that day, Matt seemed to be unaffected by his foam-wrapped hand; he caught passes just as well as he had in other games. He ran his routes with speed and intensity and used the foam on the one hand to guide the ball into his other hand and make each catch.

Telling Stephanie about these memories brought a spirit of admiration and respect for Matt as we drove. I was anxious to find the deeper story behind him. When we arrived, Matt and his wife, Shannon, greeted us at the door and treated us as honored guests, telling us we would have to stay after the interview for dinner. Their two boys, five-year-old Crew and three-year-old Graham, played and shared toys with our daughter throughout the interview.

Before directing specific questions to Matt, I explained to Shannon and him the idea behind this book—what a "spiritual warrior" was, in my mind. It was interesting to see how well Shannon understood the concept; she had worked with young women in her ward and could see that there was a fight and courage within them, even when they sometimes didn't live up to that inner greatness. What she said impressed me.

Shannon: "The youth of this generation are going to be something special someday, for better or worse. They'll become either really good or really bad. There's no mediocrity. You don't survive if you're on middle ground anymore. I know someone at BYU who totally had a warrior spirit; he was an incredible missionary, but afterward he developed such a chip on his shoulder. He came to BYU, but everybody thought he stretched the limits of what LDS people should look like. He just had this really creative spirit. He became bitter toward some members of the Church, which was partly his fault for thinking everybody was overly critical. He was an amazing missionary, so I knew he had a testimony, but he did go through that rough patch. He's doing great now, and I think of people like him when I think of warriors. If people could have heard the stories I heard about his mission, they would have known who he really was.

"You just can't judge—we have to support and keep inviting people like that and find ways to relate to them. I see that in the young women so much. There is greatness inside, but they'll go through stages when they have bad attitudes. Over the years, people at church will label them, and overcoming such labels is hard. So I think a lot of people have that inner warrior but turn away from it, and it's not at all because they don't know Jesus Christ is their Savior. They just let other people get in the way of the Savior, allowing those people to depress their greatness. They begin to feel like they don't have a place within the Church.

"When we lived in Provo, I heard some great counsel in a leadership training meeting. It's so applicable to anyone who's struggling and has that warrior spirit. The challenge was this: Find out who you really are inside; take a moment and find a quiet place for prayer. Really, sincerely ask Heavenly Father how He feels about you. If you desire it, He will pour out His Spirit and let you know you're His loved son or daughter. Once you have that kind of assurance, you can say, 'Okay, I know this. I can move forward. I can go be who God wants me to be.'"

In Doctrine and Covenants 42:61, the Lord told Joseph Smith, "If thou shalt ask, thou shalt receive revelation upon revelation, knowledge upon knowledge, that thou mayest know the mysteries and peaceable things—that which bringeth joy, that which bringeth life eternal."

I was so impressed with Shannon and her ability to understand the inner struggle youth sometimes have if they don't recognize that potential within themselves.

I turned to Matt and asked him how the Lord prepared him to be a leader at BYU.

Matt: "My dad's currently a stake president in Phoenix, Arizona. They were splitting the stake, so Elder Neil L. Anderson came, and he brought the Phoenix mission president and his wife with him. The mission president's wife said something that always comes to mind when I think of leadership: 'There's no growth in comfort zones, and there's no comfort in growth zones.' That's really stuck with me. When Heavenly Father wants you to be a leader, you get thrown into situations that will make you feel uncomfortable.

"For example, when I was younger, my Young Men's leader called me once and said, 'We need to go and invite so-and-so to church. I'm going to come pick you up, and we'll go over together.' I didn't know this young man well, but we knocked on the door, and my leader said 'Okay, invite him to church.' I asked, 'What do I say?' He simply responded, 'Say whatever comes to you.' I had to go by the Spirit. Situations like this helped me to learn to rely on the Spirit and develop the gift of leadership.

"I attended Cactus High School in Peoria, Arizona, and most people were of other faiths, so only a handful of the guys I hung out with were members of the Church. Even though we believed in different things, we all got along really well. High school football can be a rough atmosphere, so I did my best to avoid the bad things. After my sophomore year, however, it became more difficult because I was thrown into the spotlight. [Matt was the leading receiver for the varsity team his sophomore year.] I started getting invited to all the big parties. I knew there was a lot of underage drinking and questionable activities going on at these parties. When people started inviting me, I had to make the decision quickly to not put myself into those situations. People began to learn my standards and the decisions I made. Eventually, when anyone tried to get me to do bad things, my friends would essentially answer for me. They would stick up for me: 'Don't offer that to him. He doesn't do that.' Most were not members of the Church, but they had caught on to my standards and respected me for them. They were fighting my battles for me! It was great.

"Those decisions I made when I was younger really molded me. I could have made the decision to just try a party or two out. My friends were there; I could go hang with them. I wouldn't do anything wrong. But you can't do that. There's no way I would have been 'standing in holy places' [D&C 87:8] if I had been there. There's no telling what sorts of temptations would have been there, and one may have been the perfect temptation for me. The devil does that with temptations; he's very cunning, manufacturing the perfect temptation for you.

"But like I said, by the time my senior year rolled around, my friends were protecting me. They didn't believe the same things I believed, but they respected my beliefs and were on my side. If I could give any advice to youth, I would say that so much of what you become has to do with your friends. Choose them wisely. You're never forced into any group of friends just because of what you look like or what you do. Seek out the people who will best influence you and be friends with them."

After Christ fasted for forty days, "the tempter came to him" (Matthew 4:3). Satan sought to catch Jesus in His physical weakness. Jesus refused the first temptation, but "then the devil came unto him" (JST Matthew 4:6) again, attempting a different approach. Christ once again withstood the temptation. For the third time, "the devil came unto him again, and said, All these things [the riches of the world] will I give thee, if thou wilt fall down and worship me" (JST Matthew 4:9). The Savior responded to the adversary, "Get thee hence, Satan: for it is written, Thou shalt worship the Lord thy God, and him only shalt thou serve. Then the devil leaveth him, and, behold, angels came and ministered unto him" (Matthew 4:10–11).

It's interesting to see that by three consecutive choices against temptation, Jesus made a statement to Lucifer that He would not be broken. Lucifer withdrew. These three consecutive choices also granted Jesus the company of angels. In a similar way, Matt's consistent refusal to attend the wrong parties made a statement. The temptations eventually withdrew, and Matt was granted the company of mortal "angels" who may not have belonged to the same religion, but found unity in Christianity and felt it was their duty to help protect Matt's values.

Matt: "Out of high school, I was being recruited heavily by a particular university. I went there on a recruiting trip, and they offered me a scholarship. I was excited; they knew how to appeal to me as a receiver. We watched a highlight film that showed how much they pass, how much they love the deep ball. As a seventeen-year-old kid, it sounded awesome. My dad came with me, and I remember him saying, 'This will be really hard to turn down.'

"On recruiting trips, the current players for the university take you out and show you a good time. The first night they took us out, I think we ended up going to some sort of a pizza place where there were some drinks served. I declined, and they were cool with it. They knew I was a member of the Church. Then we started heading to a party, and I said, 'Eh, let's go back early.' They were fine with it and took me back to the hotel.

"The next night, they took us out, and we ate. Then we started heading somewhere else. 'Where are we going?' I asked. 'Oh, we're going to a strip club.' I said, 'I don't think we should go there.' They all said things like, 'Oh, come on. It'll be fine.'

'I'm only seventeen. They won't let me in.' I tried to pull that card. They responded, 'It's fine. We know some people who'll let you in.' We pulled up to the place, and something inside me said, 'You have to make a decision and make it now. Otherwise, it's going to be too late.' I said, 'You know, I'm sorry to spoil the party; can you take me back to the hotel?' The guy driving didn't hesitate—he was kind about it and took me home. In fact, he called me afterward and said, 'Hey, we'll come pick you up; we're going to go hang out at the beach.' I remember them taking me back to the hotel and my dad being there. I told him what was going on and that I had decided it wasn't for me.

"I don't think their football program was bad. I just think that at that moment, I had to make the right decision, and from that point on it's been a lot easier to make decisions like that one. That was a crossroad in my life. Had I not made that decision, it might have affected me forever. It was hard because it was just me—I didn't have my friends from high school around me that time. I had to make a stand for myself. But it got easier once I had made up my mind."

Shannon: "If you hadn't made that decision, nobody would have ever found out."

Matt: "Yeah, I could have hidden that from most people."

That little decision led to signing with BYU—a big difference in Matt's future career (see Alma 37:6). In the eyes of the world, decisions like this would make Matt look weak, like he was too soft. However, in the eyes of God, this decision made Matt a warrior. It did not matter, to the Lord, if Matt was seen as weak. "I call upon the weak things of the world, those who are unlearned and despised, to thresh the nations by the power of my Spirit" (D&C 35:13). These decisions prepared Matt for missionary work. Matt trained with the Cougars for a season, and then left on his mission.

Matt: "I served in the Samoa Apia Mission. The Lord calls the meek to serve as His mouthpiece, and the weak things of the world become great. We had an island-wide conference with the mission president, President Pe'a, the first day of my mission. I had just come in with a new group of missionaries.

"President Pe'a called me up and said, 'In your eyes, these new missionaries may be weak. But one day, Elder Allen is going to be a great leader in this mission.' I had only met the mission president two hours before, so that was interesting, but I didn't think much of it. I thought, *That was really nice of him to see me on the front row and remember my name like that.*

"I got transferred the next day to another island, Tutuila, on American Samoa. We had another island conference for this particular island, with an Area Authority leading the conference this time. He had never met me, but he called me up and said the same thing—that I was going to be a great leader among the missionaries. I thought this was a strange coincidence; I wanted to do my best to fulfill whatever was going on and be the best missionary I could be. I could never get that out of my mind.

"Youth are told all the time how much potential they have. Some take that message and believe it, working toward their potential. Others take a passive approach and say, 'Well, I probably do have great potential, but I'm just going to take whatever comes to me.' Others might not even believe, saying, 'I'm not the one with potential,' because of this reason or that reason. Or, 'I'm not that great.' But I dedicated myself to becoming whatever it was those two leaders saw in me. There were times when I struggled, but I learned many things from all those experiences.

"I had been in the mission field for three and a half or four months, and we had a baptism in our area. The baptism was on Saturday and the confirmation on Sunday in sacrament meeting. We had an excellent ward mission leader named Brother Fano.

"We must not have communicated with him well; we went up to give the confirmation, and nobody knew who was supposed to perform the ordinance. So on the spot, Brother Fano looked at me and said, 'Elder Allen, why don't you do it?' It really, really caught me off guard. I said, 'I don't speak very good Samoan; I don't think I could.'

He said, 'That's fine; do it in English.' I said, 'No, I think I'd be more comfortable if somebody else did it.' I declined and somebody else did it. I went away from that thinking, *What did I just do? I was offered the privilege of performing a priesthood ordinance, and I said no.* I couldn't believe myself.

"The following week, Brother Fano came over to our house. He was mostly talking to my native companion, and then he turned to me and said, 'Elder Allen, you don't speak very good Samoan, do you?' I was a little bit offended, but I had already told him the same thing, and I knew what he was getting at and why he was saying that. I thought, *He's disappointed in me for not stepping up. I'm disappointed in myself as well.*

"Later that same week, he came to our house, grabbed us, and said, 'There's a young boy in the hospital and he's really sick.' I was picking this up in bits and pieces, but I understood overall what he was saying. I'm not sure what illness this boy had, but Brother Fano told us we were going to the hospital and giving him a blessing. On the way over, I finally picked up that this boy, who was nine or ten, wasn't a member of the Church. His immediate family wasn't either, but extended family had offered to arrange a priesthood blessing, and they had accepted.

"The boy was in the ICU. We got to the room, and I had never seen so many lines and tubes hooked up to anybody before in my life. He didn't respond at all. There were about eight or nine family members in the small room, most of whom were not members of the Church, so it was an intimidating situation. This was a chance not only to perform our priesthood duty but also help nonmembers feel the power of the priesthood as well. Once again, I went in there without any expectation of doing anything myself; I was the new guy and didn't speak the language well. Brother Fano, without giving me an opportunity to decline this time, said, 'Okay, Elder Nun Yan, you're going to anoint him. Elder Allen, you're going to seal the anointing.' I wasn't even given a choice.

"I knew all the right words to say to complete the blessing, seal the anointing, and close, but besides that, I don't remember what I said. I know that I said something—I think it was coherent, and I think at least some people understood me. I finished, thinking, *I did it; no matter what happens, I did it.* I found out later that the boy made a full recovery, left the hospital the next day, and was in school just two days after that.

"That was the point in my life when I realized how real the priesthood is. The Lord will accomplish His purposes, and we are His tools. It has nothing to do with the words of the blessing; it has everything to do with the faith of those involved. This family had so much faith in a foreigner they didn't know—they didn't even know the religion well. I think it had a lot to do with the faith of Brother Fano too; I think he knew exactly what he was doing. It was a real testimony builder to me. I'm always going to remember that experience. There's no way I can ever deny the power of the Lord. He was able to practically raise someone from the dead. From that time forward, I never hesitated. Whether it was a priesthood blessing, teaching, or speaking in Samoan in any situation—I decided to never second-guess an opportunity to do good for others.

"What my mission president and the Area Authority had said about my leadership began to be fulfilled. After about eight months, a situation occurred, and they needed a new zone leader. They called me to fill that vacancy, and I served there for about three months. Then it was time for President Pe'a to go home. The next mission president was going to be an American who had served in Samoa as a young man.

"About a month and a half before the change in mission presidents, the assistants came to our door and said, 'Pack your bags; you're going to be transferred,' but they wouldn't tell me where I was going to serve. The next day, President Pe'a called me to be his new assistant. I would serve with him for a month and a half so that by the time the new president came, I would be ready to help him run things. Again, I remember thinking, *I don't think I'm ready for it.*

"I feel like the Lord may have been preparing me for future leadership. I learned so much about the Church and how to be a leader—not just in the Church but also in the community. There are two countries in my mission, so we had to work a lot with Samoan government officials. It was the same lesson I had gone through when I was younger: I had a duty. I'd never done it before, but it was what I was supposed to do. Go and do it. I learned to rely on the Spirit and figure out what to do through promptings."

"Samoa has a rich culture of tribes and chiefs. It has a hierarchy—the people really respect parents, grandparents, and especially chiefs. You learn as a missionary how to give speeches; speeches have cultural significance. When you knock on a door, you stand and give a speech asking permission to enter the home. The higher up the chief's rank, the more flowery the speech should be.

"I remember one day with President Pe'a. We went into a house, and I was thinking, *Okay, this is a high chief of this village, as are the other men with him.* I was the only white guy in the room. They gave a speech to welcome us, and President Pe'a turned to me and said, 'Elder Allen, go ahead and respond to the speech.' In the moment, what do you do? You step up and say whatever comes to you.

"Little things like that helped me develop leadership—learning to rise up when I was called upon instead of cowering away. I was able to say what I needed to, and we were able to establish a friendship with those tribal leaders."

"Go ye therefore, and teach all nations, baptizing them in the name of the Father, and of the Son, and of the Holy Ghost: Teaching them to observe all things whatsoever I have commanded you: and, lo, I am with you alway, even unto the end of the world" (Matthew 28:19–20).

Matt faithfully completed his mission. Almost immediately upon returning home, Matt's uncle helped shape his near future with a poignant insight regarding a passage from the Doctrine and Covenants: "He that receiveth me receiveth my Father; and he that receiveth my Father receiveth my Father's kingdom; therefore all that my Father hath shall be given unto him" *(D&C 84:37–38; emphasis added).*

Matt: "We've been promised, as God's children, to receive all that He has. All we have to do is obey His commandments and we are promised everything He can give. My cousin and I left on our missions around the same time. When we got home, we all met as an extended family, and my cousin and I reported on our missions. Uncle Steve pulled us aside and gave some advice about our futures.

"He said, 'You have within you the power of God, and God has promised you everything He has. He wants to give you everything—not just eternally, in this life as well. But you have to be courageous enough to do what He wants you to do. It won't just come to you. You have to put your faith in action and work to get what Heavenly Father has in store for you.'

"I've remembered that my whole life. There are times when I lose sight of it and end up settling for something less than what Heavenly Father wants for me. But overall, my uncle's advice has stuck with me. We can have everything our Heavenly Father has, but it's up to us and our faith to actively seek it."

Matt then returned to BYU, determined to follow his uncle's advice in academics, football, and pursuing and establishing a future family and career.

Matt: "I met Shannon just a couple of weeks after returning to BYU in April 2003. My aunt set us up on a blind date, and we instantly became good friends. We dated throughout my redshirt season, and to this day Shannon claims that I deceived her, because as a redshirt [redshirts don't play in games] I had no obligations on the weekends. To her, dating a football player seemed like a typical relationship experience. Little did she realize that for the next four seasons, I'd rarely be around on the weekends because of various football commitments I had to keep.

"We were married in the Mesa Arizona Temple in the spring before my freshman season. Luckily, even with busy weekends, we found time to draw closer to each other during the first few years of our marriage.

"I had been recruited out of high school by Coach Lavell Edwards and his staff; I thought that was pretty cool because he was a legend. I was actually still in Provo—I hadn't left yet on my mission—when they made the coaching change. He retired, and I was on campus when Coach Gary Crowton came and took over, right before my mission. Such a good guy, with a phenomenal offensive mind. He did a really good job.

"I got back from my mission and joined the team again. But we had a couple of losing seasons. There were a lot of individuals on the team; we weren't united at all. Things happened, and Coach Mendenhall took over. He'll be the first to tell you about the spiritual experiences he had—different experiences he drew strength and encouragement from.

"I remember when he started involving the Spirit in conversations with football. We started praying before our meetings. I thought, *Why have we* not *been praying?* After all, it was a unique school, owned by the Church. We hadn't done any of that before then, and nobody seemed to miss it. I asked myself, 'Why didn't I think of that? Why would we *not* be praying for the success of this team, for our teammates, and for the school?'"

FOR IF YE WOULD HEARKEN UNTO THE SPIRIT WHICH TEACHETH A MAN TO PRAY, YE WOULD KNOW THAT YE MUST PRAY; FOR THE EVIL SPIRIT TEACHETH NOT A MAN TO PRAY, BUT TEACHETH HIM THAT HE MUST NOT PRAY. BUT BEHOLD, I SAY UNTO YOU THAT YE MUST PRAY ALWAYS, AND NOT FAINT; THAT YE MUST NOT PERFORM ANY THING UNTO THE LORD SAVE IN THE FIRST PLACE YE SHALL PRAY UNTO THE FATHER IN THE NAME OF CHRIST, THAT HE WILL CONSECRATE THY PERFORMANCE UNTO THEE, THAT THY PERFORMANCE MAY BE FOR THE WELFARE OF THY SOUL. (2 NEPHI 32:8–9)

Matt: "There were certain spiritual things Coach Mendenhall saw that we lacked. He believed those things affected how we performed in the classroom and on the field. A light went on for me at that point. The fact that Coach Mendenhall has been having so much success doesn't surprise me at all. I attribute a lot of that to his faith. It causes his players to build faith—not just in the program or in themselves, but also in the Savior and in the role that He can have in their success.

"I had a couple of experiences during that time that were great testimony builders. One happened when Zac Collie approached me in the training room. He was a good friend, probably my best friend on the team. Something was wrong with his hip; the doctors thought that it was a hairline fracture. He was trying to earn a starting position and a scholarship, but he wasn't able to participate because of hip pain. I remember one afternoon right after practice, he said, 'Matt, could you help give me a blessing?' That was surprising to me at first; I had never given a blessing in a football training room. He pulled me into one of the offices, and Ryan Slater was there to give the blessing. I wouldn't have chosen anyone else. Ryan Slater was the epitome of what a BYU student athlete should be.

"I remember thinking, *What other organization has so many young men like Ryan Slater—ready and worthy to give a priesthood blessing?* Besides the University of Utah and maybe some other Utah schools, what other football team could have such a unique experience? I thought, *Why* wouldn't *we be doing this? Why* wouldn't *we give a blessing to help him with an injury?* In the grand scheme of things, I don't think football is really that important to Heavenly Father, but He has set His power apart for us to use and bless those who're afflicted. I really appreciated the faith Zac had to ask us. I remember feeling the Spirit so strongly, in the training room of the football facility. It was such a cool experience."

The Spirit was incredibly strong at this point in our interview. I began to explain the conversation I'd had with Coach Mendenhall, and that Coach had called Matt one of the warriors of the team. I asked him how he had channeled that warrior spirit into doing positive, uplifting things. His response was interesting. It revealed that Matt's personality was different from Markell's and John's, and yet all three had become equally courageous warriors.

Matt: ". . . I played the wrong sport."

Shannon (laughing): "I have never thought of Matt as being the 'warrior' type—he's always so calm and collected! The whole time you were using the term *warrior*, I don't know . . . I was just thinking, *Not Matt*."

Matt (laughing): "I've never had the mentality of 'I'm a warrior! I have to take out my aggression on the football field!'"

Shannon: "When I think of warriors, I think of Cameron Jensen or Bryan Kehl."

Matt: "Yeah, exactly. I'm not a Cameron Jensen, a Bryan Kehl, or a Shaun Nua."

Shannon (asking Matt): "So then why would Bronco consider you a warrior? What do you think he sees? [Turned again to me.] Because I think Coach Mendenhall has a lot of respect for Matt. I know he thinks highly of Matt. He's not an aggressive person, but he has an unconquerable spirit. He's consistent and unwavering. Maybe that's what Coach saw. When I think of Captain Moroni, I think of Matt. He only gets mad when people do wrong things. I don't think of either Captain Moroni or Matt as fierce men. I think of them as leaders—consistent and unwavering."

Matt: "I don't think I have a fierce or dominating attitude. There's nothing about me that says I'm a warrior. But you mentioned spirit, and I think that's where it can be applicable. Having a warrior spirit means never giving up. In football, we come together as a team, like an army that trains together. Everybody's got each other's backs; we'd do anything for one another. We have that relentless spirit of never giving up, no matter what we're doing. Warrior spirits won't stop until either they're dead or their cause has been won. There will be people who try to tell such spirits what they can or can't do, but regardless, the warriors don't stop until they accomplish what they set out to do.

"I love Teancum and his warrior spirit. He was so fearsome, but he would've done anything for his people. He risked his life so many times, never thinking of himself. He thought less about his own life than he did for his people and their freedom [Alma 62:37].

That might have been what Coach saw in me: I was rarely on the sidelines yelling, 'Put me in.' I wanted to play if I could help the team, but I think I cared more about my teammates than myself. There were so many great guys on that team, and they were great influences on me. Just being able to see them succeed, and succeeding together, was probably a bigger thrill than my own success. So maybe that was the warrior characteristic Coach saw in me."

Though Matt focused more on the team's collective success than on his own stats, his were still impressive. During Matt's career, he had eighty catches for 1,076 yards and eight touchdowns. This included a twenty-eight-yard touchdown catch against Utah and a game-winning touchdown catch against New Mexico in 2005, and six catches and 108 receiving yards against Boston College in 2006. His senior year, he was a finalist for the prestigious Wuerffel Trophy, honoring the college football player who best combines exemplary community service with athletic and academic achievement.

With his success, Matt maintained a team-oriented attitude, never seeming to let it get to his head. To the contrary, the last part of our interview revealed that he had almost felt unworthy of so many blessings. He felt a responsibility to somehow give back—because "he [had] more abundantly he should impart more abundantly" (Mosiah 18:27).

Matt: "There was an experience I had with the team that became an *aha* moment for me. My sophomore year, in 2005, Coach Mendenhall had the idea of doing firesides before the games. He wanted to do something more uplifting than what we had been doing before. We used to bus everybody to a movie theater or just stay in the hotel the night before a game. We watched some really lame movies. He thought, *There has to be a better way to prepare.* So he presented the idea of holding a BYU football fireside to some stakes in San Diego, and essentially they responded, 'We have a lot of firesides as it is; we don't know if people will show.' So it didn't happen in San Diego. That weekend, we played one of the worst games that I can recall."

Shannon: "That was a terrible game!"

Matt: "Worst game I've ever played in. The next game was at the University of New Mexico. At this point, we had one win and three losses. Our only win was against Eastern Illinois, which is a Division 1 Double-A school.

"Coach Mendenhall had coached in New Mexico, so he was more familiar with some of the Church leaders in the area and was able to set up a fireside. It was sparsely attended. He left it open to the players whether we would go or stay at the hotel, and not many of us went to the fireside either. We did get a win that game—not to attribute our win to the fireside, but it was an interesting correlation."

Shannon: "That was a turning point in Coach Mendenhall's career, I think."

Matt: "It was a turning point. More and more people started to attend those firesides, and more and more players started going too. I went to every one after that. It was interesting to see a different side of these football players, who were really hardcore warriors on the field. These were tough guys; we definitely had some warriors on the team there. So to see these guys' softer, spiritual sides, I got a glimpse of who they really were underneath. The firesides became a huge deal. Coach Mendenhall was using the football program as an avenue to teach the gospel.

"Halfway through that season, Coach Doman asked if any of the team captains would be willing to take charge of organizing the firesides. I jumped at the opportunity.

"I felt I owed it to the Lord. I grew up in a great family; my parents and all my siblings are athletic. Athleticism came naturally to me. I worked hard as a high school athlete, but I wasn't a gym rat or anything like that. I wouldn't say I was Rudy, working my way up from the bottom. I was always talented—the fastest guy in high school. Once I got to college, I started thinking, *I've pretty much been handed something that millions of other people don't have.* And I wondered, *Why? Why did Heavenly Father choose me?*

"In our society, it's such a desirable thing to be athletic. People look up to BYU football players. They're highly regarded for what they do. I felt like I hadn't done anything extraordinary to earn it, so when Coach Mendenhall started doing the firesides, it really hit me that this was our chance to do something because of what we'd been given. It was a way to use our talents to serve others. If I could use the gifts I had been given to help somebody else in their testimony, of course I would. Why *wouldn't* we be doing this?

"We had some great firesides. It was a great way to prepare, not just for a football game, but also the young football players to be better fathers, missionaries, and leaders. Each week, we'd ask for two volunteers to speak. I never had an empty slot; players would volunteer week after week. The talks were amazing story after amazing story. Players who weren't members of the Church wanted to speak; they talked about the opportunities they'd had at BYU, and what a great place it was because of the Holy Ghost. For a while, it was a struggle to get musical numbers set up, so Shannon said, 'Why don't you all sing

'The Army of Helaman' song?' So we tried it. Half of us didn't know how to sing that well, but together, I think we sounded pretty strong. Cameron Jensen was talented on the piano. I think it turned out to be a pretty powerful thing; we had big, strong football players singing their testimonies.

"We discovered we could be warriors through missionary work. I felt so strongly about all of it. I remember thinking, *Maybe this is why. Maybe this is why I've had these athletic talents, so that I could be in a position where other people can listen to what I have to say.* Many times, what catches people's attention first are on-the-field accomplishments. If we could use that to draw people into what our real message is, what a great tool that would be! The firesides were some of the greatest experiences I had with BYU."

Matt graduated with a degree in exercise science and a minor in business management in 2007. He then enrolled at the University of Southern California and graduated in 2011 with a doctorate in physical therapy. After completing his one-year residency in Temecula, California, he became the director of physical therapy of an outpatient orthopedic clinic located in Fallbrook, California. He and Shannon now have three boys and enjoy watching them play sports, taking their family out to play at the beach, and serving in their ward and stake.

SHANE HUNTER

"But charity is the pure love of Christ, and
it endureth forever" (Moroni 7:47).

*O*ne of the warriors on my list was my childhood friend
Shane Hunter. We played Little League football together
in Idaho and at Snow College. We ended up being teammates at BYU as well. Throughout my childhood, I was able to learn
from his leadership. I remember him being so enthusiastic about football. I felt I could follow Shane into war. He was an inspiring captain
for our Little League football team in Idaho Falls. When high school
came along, my family moved, and Shane and I played on rival high
schools against each other. I remember being amused when our coaches
warned us about "Hunter," and we planned our schemes around him!
After high school, Shane and I were recruited by Snow College, and we
went to play together.

I remember a specific incident at Snow that inspired me forever. At the beginning of our freshman season, we were only back-
ups. The backup players hardly played in games at all—we were used
mostly in practice. I had considered myself an all-star, and it hurt my
pride to be assigned to the second team. I remember getting discouraged and going through the motions during practices. After all, what
difference could a backup player make? Our job was basically to give
the starters a break when they got tired at practice.

Shane was still excited about the prospect of playing football, second team or starting team. I remember his contagious enthusiasm. I recall a specific practice when two of the offensive linemen made excellent blocks, creating an opening for their running back. If the running back made that hole, he would run right past us defensive players for a touchdown.

Shane must have spotted that opening quickly; he shot into it like a bullet at the exact same time the running back did. Helmets and shoulder pads popped under the impact. The impact from Shane's hit to the running back's upper body was so sudden and unexpected that he almost did a complete backflip, midair before he hit the ground. Coach Steve Coburn, who I admired for passion, came screaming onto the field, congratulating Shane.

Next Saturday, game day, Shane was a starter. I remembered the feeling he'd electrified us with in practice, and I planted it in my soul. If I nurtured that seed of enthusiasm, I could make the starting team too. I'd have to play with the excitement and fervor of a starter and abandon my discouraged attitude. I worked hard to have a Shane-like attitude every single practice, and several games later I became a starter too.

Two years later, I was halfway into my mission. I was serving in Paysandú, one of the larger cities in Uruguay. My comp and I didn't have a single investigator to teach. We worked hard—contacting in the streets, stopping people while shopping, knocking on doors—but nobody seemed interested. Our lessons were confined to the less-active members. Again, I had a complaining heart. I said to myself, "We should be teaching investigators. Why are we teaching less-active members?" It's hard to admit, but I remember feeling bored during those lessons.

One night in a dream, I revisited, in perfect clarity, Shane's tackle as a backup linebacker. The dream was so vivid; I believe the Holy Ghost brought it to my mind. I saw and experienced everything I had experienced two years ago at Snow College. I saw myself going heartlessly through the plays. I saw Shane play with excitement and passion. I saw, heard, and almost felt the bone-chilling hit on that running back. I saw Coach Coburn sprint to Shane from the sideline, screaming in excitement. I woke up with a clear message: "If you want to be a starter, play with passion, as if you were a starter. If you want to teach investigators, teach with passion, as if you were teaching investigators, for less-active members of the Church are every bit as precious as investigators are."

I recognized my fault and began to pray. I realized God loves all His children, whether new to the Church or less active, and repented earnestly for being unenthusiastic. I realized that a lack of excitement, in any setting, stifles progression. A love, a fervor for life causes good things to "work together for your good" (D&C 105:40), and opportunities for greatness come naturally. It's a principle applicable to football, applicable to missionary work, and applicable to literally anything else in life.

Consider the story of Ammon. It was gratitude and excitement that helped him take advantage of a dangerous situation. King Lamoni's sheep were being scattered by a rival group of Lamanites. If Ammon and his fellow servants didn't gather the sheep back together, Lamoni would put them to death. Notice the understandable attitude of the king's servants: "Now the servants of the king began to murmur, saying: Now the king will slay us, as he has our brethren because their flocks were scattered by the wickedness of these men. And they began to weep exceedingly, saying: Behold, our flocks are scattered already. Now they wept because of the fear of being slain" (Alma 17:28–29). This was a situation where anyone would have a defeated attitude. The king was going to kill them. It seems like Ammon should have been discouraged too. He had come to live amongst the Lamanites as a missionary and was now facing death for his service as a sheepherder.

But Ammon was excited to be in this grave situation. "Now when Ammon saw this his heart was swollen within him with joy; for, said he, I will show forth my power unto these my fellow-servants, or the power which is in me, in restoring these flocks unto the king, that I may win the hearts of these my fellow-servants, that I may lead them to believe in my words" (Alma 17:29). That kind of optimism seems borderline crazy!

Though Shane's example isn't as extreme, his excitement for being nothing more than a second-team linebacker reflects the attitude of Ammon. He was grateful and excited for the opportunity that a challenge brought to him. He was glad to prove to the coaches that he was more than a second-team player. I believe it was this attitude that brought Shane from being a second-team player at a junior college to being an all-conference player at a Division 1 university.

This is the attitude of a true warrior. Shane has since gone through some extremely difficult things, but I've always observed him relishing life and being grateful for what he has.

Shane and I have always been friends. My wife, Stephanie, and his wife, Carrie, had also been good friends at Snow College. He was working down at Snow College as a football coach at the time I called him for an interview. He told me he was planning to come to Provo and visit family with his wife and two-year-old daughter, Halle. We arranged for them to stop by our house beforehand. Stephanie and I were both excited to see our old friends.

Shane isn't exceptionally tall (at five feet ten inches), but his shoulders are as broad as he is tall. He is a solid block of hard-hitting iron. He would have been intimidating if I didn't already know him. I knew his spirituality far outweighed his physical size. In the few days preceding the interview, I pondered the intensity he had taught me at Snow. I wanted to know where it came from, so I started out by asking him where he first developed leadership.

Shane: "I always tried to take on the example of the people around me. I would watch people I really admired and apply what they did. My dad was always one of those people. He didn't tell you what to do; he showed you what to do. Every once in a while, he would have to be vocal, but he understood that being a great example is just to show the way. He never tried to push people. He just encouraged them a lot. I tried to follow his example.

"I don't know if I will ever reach what he had, but he had an amazing work ethic. Nothing was below him. It didn't matter what job it was. It could have been emptying garbage or doing something *big* that gets more praise. No matter to him—it was the same job. If it needed to be done, he was going to do it. That's the attribute that sticks out in my mind: how hard he did everything. He worked full-time, always trying really hard when he was at work, but he also made time to coach us kids in the sports we played.

"Another attribute I admired was his love. He didn't think negatively about others. He was nice to everyone; it didn't matter if it was a co-worker or somebody he had met on the street. He was that person's best friend instantly. He was able to talk. He cared. He had been through his own share of trials in his life and was able to relate to all kinds of different people.

"The loves I learned from him were the love of family, of people, and of sports. He also taught me to take those feelings and apply them to everything I did. I love football. Dad always taught me that it was a team game; it was never just for me. I could be a great player, but unless I worked as a team, it didn't matter. He taught me early on to help bring everybody else along.

"Out of everyone I knew, my dad was my hero. As far as the scriptures, I think everyone's favorite is Captain Moroni. I love the scriptures about him; I admire the love he had for his people and his desire for them to be better [Alma 48:11]. He had a great understanding of their relationship to God, and he wanted them to understand their divine potential. I think that he's one of the most amazing examples. Another hero for me is the prophet Ether because of what he went through. Knowing the love he had for his people, not being able to preach to them must have been frustrating. They had become so hard in their hearts that they wouldn't accept the gospel. My favorite scripture is Ether 12:6: 'Ye receive no witness until after the trial of your faith.' That's been my favorite scripture for as long as I can remember. Nothing is easy; if it is, then it's probably not worth it. Working hard for something makes it that much better when you accomplish it. That scripture really sticks out to me.

"The examples of people like that helped me develop leadership, and a great place to practice that leadership was in sports.

"I've played football as far back as I can remember. I have an older brother, Adam, and he was always playing. He would bring his friends over, and we would go play at school, so even at a young age I was around football, and I got the chance to develop pretty quickly. Later, when I played with kids from my age group, I had a chance to help them.

"That helped me to understand love a little more. At that time, I thought it was just the love of football—wanting to win. It incorporated more than that, though. I wanted those guys playing with me to understand the game. I wanted them to feel like I did—about football and about working together as a team.

"During high school, football taught me a lot about overcoming aggression. In football, you want to lash out sometimes. Someone does something to you, and you get upset on the inside. For me, I physically want to do something about it. I physically want to let that person know, 'That's not right,' or, 'I don't like what you just did.' It's hard to suppress, but if you channel those feelings of aggression into a more noble feeling like determination, you can use it. You'll have a greater focus on what you are trying to accomplish. I try to do that, especially during a game, whether it's something that someone said to me or because I didn't do well. It makes me more focused on the next play. Next chance I get, I have to do well. I have to do my job exactly right. I clear all the distractions from my mind and put the next play into focus.

"Have goals. Understand what you want. Have a vision of what you want life to be. Life is tough; bad things are going to happen, so take those things, learn from them, and then apply them to what you're trying to do.

"The second game of my junior year, we were playing against Madison High School. Somehow, during the course of the game, I lost feeling in my left leg. From the knee down, I couldn't feel anything. I finished the game, but we lost. We started with an 0–2 record that year. I was depressed; junior year is the first time you really start on varsity, and you want to make it awesome. You dream about it as a kid. We just weren't doing well, and my leg was hurting. I could hardly use it during the second half, but I did everything I could to play. That night, I was probably in the most pain I've ever been in. I couldn't do anything because my leg hurt so bad.

"The next day, we went to the doctor, and I found out I had anterior compartment syndrome. It ended up basically paralyzing my leg from the knee down. I could walk a little bit, but my leg was just dead. I couldn't lift up my foot, or anything like that. That was probably one of the most traumatic physical experiences I've ever had. Things I took for granted, like just being able to walk normally, were taken away. Football, something I loved, something I could channel all my energy and efforts into, was taken away from me.

"I had a blessing from my father and a close family friend, and I was promised that things would work out. I remember lying in bed at night, trying to move my foot, thinking, *Just move!* It wouldn't. That was probably one of the biggest trials of my faith. I had been promised in that blessing that it would be okay, and nothing was happening right away. I worked at it, and eventually my foot started moving again. Near the end of the season, I was able to play again, but it still wasn't even close to normal.

"After months of rehab, I regained full mobility in my foot. I learned the Lord keeps His promises, but you have to do your part—and it takes time. That experience was hard for me, but it gave me a greater appreciation for being able to play football. I gained a greater appreciation for the gospel as well. I can't think of anything that has helped me more than that experience; it brought me to trust in the Lord. His promises are real. If we do the things He asks, trying to do everything we can, He'll keep His promises."

Shane overcame the experience, exercising trust in the Lord and channeling his frustration into determination. He became Idaho's 5A Defensive MVP his senior year. That season, he had 116 tackles, 7 interceptions, and 2 forced fumbles. A year later, Shane inspired me forever with that bone-chilling hit at Snow College to make the starting team. As soon as he became a starter, his success was immediate. He was a natural leader on our defense and soon became one of our captains. An important decision, however, came at the close of that season.

Shane: "The most important decision I made during that time was the choice to go on a mission. After my freshman football season at Snow, things were looking really good. I was a starter the second half of the season and played well. Our team looked like it was going to be pretty strong the next year; we would be able to try for a national championship. At the same time, there was something missing in my life.

"I had grown up in the Church, and my parents were great examples to me. But I hadn't decided if I truly believed with all my heart. That was the toughest decision. It would have been so easy to say, 'Well, I don't know if it's true or not, so I don't want to go.' While at Snow, I wasn't going to church as much as I had in the past. It was a spiritually tough time in my life. Then, that winter, my grandpa passed away. That really got me thinking. I wanted to know if the gospel is true. I think I had always known deep inside, but I had never really felt it in my heart.

"That's when I started reading the Book of Mormon for myself. I started praying sincerely to know if it was true, and then this all started to become real to me. I felt in my heart, 'You've always known it's true. Now you need to do it.' It was just deciding to decide. That's what helped me the most. If it was true, I knew I had to do it. I'm sure a lot of other people like me hesitate, saying, 'Well, I don't want to know if it's true, because if it is, that won't be easy.' But once you decide to decide, it makes the biggest difference. When I found out it was true, I knew that I had to go on a mission. There was no doubt. The Lord had already blessed me so much in life, and I began to recognize that. I saw what had happened in the past, like the healing of my leg, and it all became real at that point."

"Lift up your heart and rejoice, for the hour of your mission is come; and your tongue shall be loosed, and you shall declare glad tidings of great joy unto this generation" (D&C 31:3).

Shane: "I served in the North Carolina Charlotte Mission. I believe Heavenly Father gave me a love for sports—that love taught me to work hard, and hard work became a rather important preparation for the mission. Missions are hard. Whenever you go to church, everyone talks about great miracles that happened on their missions. But in reality, there are maybe five or six great miracles your whole mission long! During the seven hundred other days, you're out there getting doors slammed in your face. People yell and curse at you. There's the heart-break of seeing someone who understands the gospel chose to walk away from it. Sports prepared me for that. I had already done hard things. I think God gave me that love to teach me that if you really love something, you have to work hard for it.

"One of my favorite experiences happened in my first area. I was serving with my trainer, and we were teaching a young man who was in the military. He had grown up in rough circumstances and had done things he was not proud of. He took to the gospel quickly and wanted to learn all he could. I knew that he felt the Spirit testify to him that the gospel was true. Sadly, he never joined the Church. He wasn't willing to make the changes he needed to. The reason this is one of my favorite experiences is because of what it taught me: having a testimony is not enough. When you know that the gospel is true, you have to *do* it. That doesn't mean you'll be perfect; it just means you'll try to do your best, and when you make mistakes, you'll trust in the Atonement and strengthen your faith in Christ.

"When I think about my mission and how playing sports prepared me for it, I understand all of life works that way. Sports prepared me for my mission, sports and my mission prepared me for marriage, and marriage prepared me to be a father. That's why I'm so thankful I had that love for sports.

"I finished my mission in the fall of 2006 and came back to Snow College the following spring. Carrie and I met my first semester home from my mission. She knew some of my friends from the team, and I was introduced to her through them. We had the chance to get to know each other throughout the semester. At the end of the semester, we went on a couple of dates, and then we continued to date through-out the summer. She was living in Heber City, and I was living in Idaho Falls, so we didn't see each other as often as I would have wanted that summer. Luckily for me, she started liking me as much as I liked her, and things worked out really well when we came back to Snow in the fall.

"We continued to date through the semester, and that Christmas I decided to ask her to marry me. She came up to my house in Idaho Falls on Christmas Day and found a present waiting for her under the tree. It was the last present that had not been opened. I'm pretty sure she knew what it was. As she unwrapped the ring, I asked her if she would marry me. The happiest day of my life was February 15, 2008, when we were sealed in the Salt Lake Temple. I had just finished football with Snow and would soon be headed to play at BYU."

Shane was given a preferred walk-on position, but he was not prom-ised a scholarship. To secure a scholarship, he needed to prove himself to Coach Mendenhall. That was crucial to Shane's football dreams because without a scholarship, he'd have to quit football and get a job to pay for school. With hard work and intensity, he did catch Coach's eye. Shane was awarded a scholarship for his senior year.

Shane: "I would say one of the athletic accomplishments I'm most proud of was earning a scholarship. I came as a walk-on to BYU, earned a scholarship, and then became a starter."

Carrie: "I was pregnant, and we were tight on money. If he didn't earn that scholarship, we weren't going to be able to pay for his school. That's how big a deal it was."

Shane: "One of my favorite experiences was the game against Oklahoma [in 2009, at the new Dallas Cowboys' stadium]. Opening kickoff, I made the first tackle. Holy cow, it was unreal! The feeling of being in front of eighty thousand people and being a part of the tackle was pretty amazing. I was thinking, *That was so fast.* I mean, when you play football your whole life, it seems to slow down in your mind. But that first kickoff, I couldn't believe how fast the game was—just everybody flying by. And somehow, I ended up being right where the ball-carrier was and got the tackle. That was an amazing experience."

That game, a 14–13 victory over number three Oklahoma, started a successful season for BYU. The Cougars finished with an 11–2 record, including wins against number nineteen Utah and number twenty Oregon State in the Las Vegas Bowl. At the end of that year, many team leaders moved on to the NFL, leaving a young team behind. The following season, Shane's senior season, he and teammate Andrew Rich led the team in tackles, but the otherwise young team struggled for the first half of the year. Shane felt that it had to do with their unity.

Shane: "My senior year at BYU was a great example of how unity affects a team. We started off badly. We had a great game against Washington—the first game I started in—but then we lost four in a row. A low point was after losing to Utah State, a team BYU had dominated for so long. It honestly felt like things couldn't get much worse. Everything was going wrong. We were trying, but it just didn't seem to work.

"Everything flipped around when we came together as a team. Coach Mendenhall became the new defensive coordinator. The defense totally turned around with him. I felt like the change was instantaneous. When he took over, the hard things he made us do caused us to grow in unity and love for each other. We felt so close; we all had to do our part. In practice, Coach expected us not to let the receivers even catch the ball, and we worked up to that point. If they tried a running play, he expected us not to let them cross the line of scrimmage. He changed our whole mentality; all of us had to know exactly what our assignment was on each play, and then we had to give everything we had to get it done. That's what brought us together, and ultimately it was a successful season. Love for the game and for each other helped us understand that there was a reason behind each hard practice. Not only was it building us as football players, it was building us as people. It taught us to endure well."

Despite a 1–4 start, Coach Mendenhall's changes sparked unity and a successful remainder of the season. Mosiah 18:21: "And he commanded them that there should be no contention one with another, but that they should look forward with one eye . . . having their hearts knit together in unity and in love one towards another." The Cougars won six and lost only two of their remaining games, going on to win the New Mexico Bowl against UTEP 52–24.

Shane was given the honor to carry the Y flag out of the tunnel and onto the field for the New Mexico game. Flag-bearers are those seniors who Coach Mendenhall believes have become honorable disciples of a Church-based school. Shane made the honorable mention All-Mountain West team that year as a middle linebacker. He had the second-most tackles on the team (eighty-six) and finished his two-year career at BYU with a hundred total tackles. He picked off two passes his senior year, including one against rival Utah.

Shane: "My family became really close while I was playing at BYU. Every home-game weekend, they'd all come down from Idaho. Everyone would stay in the two-bedroom apartment Carrie and I were living in at the time. I don't have a small family by any means. Most games, there were probably four or five of my brothers and sisters there, all with their spouses and kids. They'd just sleep out on the floor Friday night, and Saturday after the game, we would all hang out. I think that brought my family together in a special way. There were no boundaries; you're sleeping next to everyone. My family and my wife got to know each other a lot more."

Shane graduated from BYU in April 2011 with a degree in exercise science. He felt a hunger for football, having only been away from the game for a semester. This helped him decide to be a coach. He began coaching at Snow College the ensuing fall football season.

It was at this time that Shane and his wife began undergoing serious trials. It began when James, Shane's father and hero, passed away from a heart attack. Shane was at football practice coaching, so Carrie had to bring him the awful news while he was at practice. James had been an amazing example of fatherhood—he had been at every game and most practices Shane had ever been involved in. He was Shane's main source of support throughout his football career.

Shane: "When it happened, I was immensely grateful for all those weekends I'd had with my family at BYU. They had brought us so close, and we were more prepared. It was still obviously difficult, but understanding what we had together, and that we would see him again, put it all into perspective. Dad had been such an example of love, and when he passed we were united enough to get through it together."

Overcoming such pain must have been incredibly difficult, and yet Shane and Carrie's trials were not over. Only six months later, Carrie's parents passed away in a car accident.

Carrie: "It was the hardest trial I've been through. I'm happy, though, to know where they are. It makes me strive harder in my marriage; I want to be like my mom and dad and have the marriage they had. Because of their example, I will not give up on marriage, no matter what happens. I will fight for what's important, even though it would be easy to fold. In the last six months, we've undergone so much tragedy, to the point where I think most marriages would drift apart. It does make trials in our marriage a lot harder, but I want to be where my parents are and where Shane's dad is. If I give up, I won't be able to see them again.

"Instead of drifting, our marriage has grown stronger in sympathy for each other. When his dad passed away, I had no clue what to say because that hadn't happened to me. I could only listen and try to make his life easier. When my parents passed, he actually knew the feeling. The comfort he's given me has increased our love for each other. Our love is something we both want to fight for; we went through all of this together."

Shane: "Two days really stick out in my memory. They helped me understand and want everything to be good with Carrie and me. It was a Monday when she came to the football field and told me that my dad had a heart attack. She told me he was in the hospital, and things weren't looking good. I saw the tears in her eyes and the pain she felt for me. I thought to myself, *That's something I never want to go through, ever.* I never wanted to tell her that something that bad had happened.

"I guess it's fate or something, but when Carrie's parents were in the accident, I was the one who got the call. I had to wake Carrie up and tell her. I told her that her mom had died and her father was in the hospital—it didn't look good for him either. I told her that our two nieces were in critical condition as well. (One of them, who was our daughter's age, ended up passing as well, but the other young girl ended up recovering miraculously.) That same feeling of complete and utter helplessness came over me.

"But with that helplessness came such a love for her. I would do anything for her. I knew she had felt exactly the same way for me. When you go through something like that together, you feel you want nothing but the best for each other. You want to do so much for each other."

Carrie: "You want somehow to never let anything bad happen to each other."

Shane: "Exactly. You just want to protect one another. It's a lot like having a newborn baby. When you hold your child in your arms for the first time, you think about that baby's life. You think if anybody ever did anything to that baby, well, you'd have a problem with that! You'd have a hard time not lashing out and protecting. You just love so much. I think it has all brought our marriage close. I do everything I can to make her understand how I feel about her. Not just to say it, but to do it."

"AND CHARITY SUFFERETH LONG . . . BEARETH ALL THINGS, BELIEVETH ALL THINGS, HOPETH ALL THINGS, ENDURETH ALL THINGS. WHEREFORE, MY BELOVED BRETHREN, IF YE HAVE NOT CHARITY, YE ARE NOTHING, FOR CHARITY NEVER FAILETH. WHEREFORE, CLEAVE UNTO CHARITY, WHICH IS THE GREATEST OF ALL, FOR ALL THINGS MUST FAIL—BUT CHARITY IS THE PURE LOVE OF CHRIST, AND IT ENDURETH FOREVER" (MORONI 7:45–47).

Carrie: "People do not realize how strong love can be. I don't think they realize—you always have strong love for at least one person. If you feel like you don't love anyone, look around. You always have a friend whom you would do anything for. That's what love is. Even when you've done something wrong, even when you don't have love in your family, there is always somebody you'd do anything for. That's love.

"In high school, I didn't get along with my parents. Back then, you wouldn't think I would've cared if I had lost them. But I would say to anyone going through similar problems: If you think you don't care, wait until you lose them. You'll realize how much you actually love them. And you might regret a lot of the things you said or did to them. You might regret ever feeling that you didn't want them in your life. You can't go through life without loving somebody or being loved. Without that love, you can't go on. Love holds everything together.

"If Shane's family didn't have so much love for one another when his dad passed, I think his family would have fallen apart. You could fall away from the gospel, from everything. You'll fall apart. I feel that's why people hurt themselves. They don't feel love."

1 John 4:18: "There is no fear in love; but perfect love casteth out fear: because fear hath torment. He that feareth is not made perfect in love."

Moroni 8:16: "Behold, I speak with boldness, having authority from God; and I fear not what man can do; for perfect love casteth out all fear."

Shane: "When I think of a warrior spirit, it's somebody who understands the greater purposes. There's a bond that draws us to greatness. That bond is love. We all have it inside. It's something that draws us toward goals. Warriors know they're going to face tough times, but love makes them capable of pushing through. Whether it's love for a friend or love for what you're doing, it's that passion and that love in their hearts that gets them through. Like Carrie said, without it, you will fall. There's no way you can make it without an understanding of the love you have inside you."

Carrie: "Since his dad passed, the way Shane has stepped up with his family has been amazing. His brother is going on a mission, and Shane wants to pay for it. That has been really big. He's set aside a lot of money to help. I think that is something his dad would have wanted him to do. He's also stepped up to comfort his mother. We try to go up to Idaho, where she lives, every single month. We want to show her our love and comfort her. He's also stepped up as a father. He's realized how important the role of a father is, and what an amazing father he had. He wants to be like him.

"Shane took on his father's leadership and love for every person, no matter who you are or what you've done. Absolute, genuine love. He never makes anyone feel lower than him in any aspect of life, even as a coach. He doesn't make the players feel like they are less than he is. They feel like they can go to him for help. That's an important attribute—to be able to make someone feel completely comfortable with you."

Shane: "Through my dad's example, I feel that the Lord has blessed me with an understanding of how to lift others up. The things I have experienced in my life—they've given me an understanding of what people are going through. I can relate to them, have empathy for them, and lift them up. The Lord has helped me see the greater individual inside them. That's why I got into coaching. I love working with kids who have no clue what their potential is. They don't see themselves as what they could become. My goal is to help them see it. It applies not just to football; it applies to life. They can be good fathers, good husbands, and good citizens in their communities."

Since our interview, Shane has become a BYU graduate-assistant coach and is enrolled in the school's Master of Public Administration program. Carrie just graduated from nursing school and is working part-time at a doctor's office. "She's a part-time nurse and a full-time mom," Shane said. Shane and Carrie have since had a son, Hudson, who is eighteen months old, and their daughter, Halle, is now four.

"We love taking our kids to the park or taking them on walks," Shane told me. "We love doing anything outdoors. Now that our baby boy, Hudson, is getting a little bit older, we'll be able to do a little bit of camping." They live in Heber, close to Carrie's family, and Shane makes the half hour commute to BYU, which he says is "fine with me, because it gives me time to relax, and it's a beautiful drive."

BRYAN KEHL

"In the fear of the Lord is strong confidence" (Proverbs 14:26).

*B*ryan Kehl is *one of the greatest spiritual leaders I've ever known. It was an honor to play with him and be inspired every time he spoke to our team as a defensive captain. It's no secret that he was the defense's most valuable player. On top of that, he was an example of how a disciple of Christ should act.*

I recall a team workout in the weight room. We had the radio on, full-volume, and an inappropriate song began to play. It was a well-known, popular song. I wondered, Is anybody going to turn it off? I know we're a Church-sponsored school, but we're football play- ers. Does anyone think twice when a song like this is played? *I thought that maybe I should turn it off, and yet I hesitated. As I listened, hesitating, the music stopped. I turned to see Bryan coming out of the volume-control room. A few players looked at him inquisitively, and I overheard him say,* "We have to remember what we represent here."

Bryan speaks in youth firesides—some of which I've attended—and he delivers powerful spiritual messages. From what I've observed in the time I played with him, he lives up to what he preaches. It's easy to speak in front of youth groups and act spiritual; it's tougher to live standards in a setting around peers. In my opinion, he does both. I sensed he was the same person whether in the weight room or in front of the pulpit.

We interviewed him in Draper, Utah, at the house he and his family stays in during the NFL off-season. I met his wife, Jessica, and even got to see his little daughter, Jayda, on the video monitor while she was sleeping. I was overjoyed to see him again. He had been my defensive captain and my spiritual example—a great leader in my life. I began the interview by asking him about his life as a child.

Bryan: "I was adopted at just two days old. From the beginning, my parents had the highest expectations for me. It's funny; there's a video of the day they adopted me. They came, picked me up, and held me, and my dad was talking about me playing in the NFL!

Jessica: "Not just the NFL—the NBA too. I thought, *They had some expectations for you.*"

Bryan: "They always believed I could do anything. So from the youngest age, I had goals of being a great athlete, and they always told me, 'Go for it.' I was so blessed with the family I had, but it was kind of interesting growing up. I'm biracial, and I was in a completely white neighborhood. That made it fun because everyone wanted to be friends with 'the black kid.' I think I always had friends because of that.

"Part of the reason I've made it so far in football is that I'm borderline dangerously confident. My wife will attest to that."

Jessica: "He does not lack in confidence at all."

Bryan: "And that's good and bad. I probably think more of myself than I should, which is bad. But I don't think confidence is all bad. It's helped me accomplish what I now have. You can't succeed in sports if you don't believe in yourself. You just can't. And I believed in myself, in part, because I was convinced I had NFL pedigree. The adoption agency told my parents that my biological father had played in the NFL as a running back, so I never doubted my ability. Whether it was in a game, in practice, or just playing around in the neighborhood, I always believed that my athletic skills were superior.

"There's a similar belief that every young person needs to have. It's important for youth to believe in what they can accomplish. Not that everyone has NFL pedigree, but we all have divine pedigree—we're all children of God and have the potential for greatness. It doesn't have to be in football or sports at all, but we're all capable of something truly great. That fact should give anyone confidence."

PSALM 82:6: "I HAVE SAID, YE ARE GODS; AND ALL
OF YOU ARE CHILDREN OF THE MOST HIGH."

Jessica: "Sometimes I wish I was as confident as he is. What would it be like? He's always so happy. When you're confident, what's there to be sad about, right? He's so fun to be around because he's secure in who he is and what he wants."

Bryan: "Confidence is so important for youth to develop. Many of the problems youth experience today deal with the desire to feel approval. They want to be respected, to be received. I honestly hope my daughter, Jayda, is almost too confident as well. I'll do my best to teach her to be confident. High school becomes much easier when you believe in yourself. Youth need to know they have worth, and that doesn't come from peers—it comes from the fact that they're children of God. They don't have to prove anything to anyone to know they're children of God.

"I wasn't always as confident as I am now. Until my sophomore year in high school, I was insecure and shy. I had an awesome bishop growing up: Bishop Silva. He was a tiny man, and maybe the most humble and giving person I ever knew. Just knowing him lifted you up. Each year, at the end of tithing settlement, he handed you your tithing statement and opened up the scriptures. One time, he said to me, 'You have just declared that you are a full tithe payer. The Lord is bound when you do what He says [D&C 82:10], and you are entitled to blessings. I want you to go home tonight, take this piece of paper, flip it over, and write on the back, 'My heart's desires.' Make a list. Don't write trivial things on there; don't be trivial with the Lord. You write down some serious blessings you desire and see if the Lord doesn't bless you.'

"So I did it, and one of the things I wrote was that I wanted to be confident and not shy anymore. If that's what changed me, I don't know, but I do know that I wasn't always as confident and secure in myself as I am now. I look at that old slip of paper still—I've kept it all these years. It's interesting because a lot of the things I wrote on it were given to me."

Bryan was incredibly successful at Brighton High School in Salt Lake as a linebacker. He was recruited by Oregon State, Utah State, Harvard, Yale, Penn, Idaho State, and of course BYU. He accepted a scholarship to the Y and played for a year before leaving on his mission. Bryan attributes this success to confidence.

When your confidence is in yourself, that confidence risks becoming pride. However, too much confidence in what the Lord can do through us is impossible. Some believe that overabundant confidence is prideful, no matter where that confidence comes from. Aaron the missionary was concerned when he heard how much confidence his brother Ammon spoke with. "Aaron rebuked him, saying: Ammon, I fear that thy joy doth carry thee away unto boasting" (Alma 26:10). Ammon's response, indicating where his confidence came from, reveals the key to having true confidence and achieving one's full potential: "I do not boast in my own strength, nor in my own wisdom; but behold, my joy is full, yea, my heart is brim with joy, and I will rejoice in my God. Yea, I know that I am nothing; as to my strength I am weak; therefore I will not boast of myself, but I will boast of my God, for in his strength I can do all things; yea, behold, many mighty miracles we have wrought in this land, for which we will praise his name forever" (Alma 26:11–12).

When Bryan described himself as "borderline dangerously confident," I thought, He's always been the most sincere, down-to-earth person. Never in my time playing with him did I ever get the impression that he thought he was better than anyone else. I disagree with his assumption that his confidence was bad. I believe his confidence was more like Ammon's than he would willingly admit. I asked him next how he balanced confidence with the commandment we all have to stay away from pride.

Bryan (laughing): "I'm still more prideful than I should be. But I try to bring it back to 'I am nothing' [Alma 26:12; see previous]. Nothing that I've done is of me. Everything I've done, everything I am is a gift. Whenever I start feeling good about myself, I try to bring it back to that fact. So even though I am extremely confident, I also recognize where it comes from. Any of my abilities, anything that I am or that I've done, I fully recognize it's not me. It's what I've been given.

"When I was on my mission in Canada, my brother Brandon sent me an inspired letter about confidence. He wrote about the story of the twelve spies, sent by Moses, to survey the promised land. The story involves two men whose confidence was in the Lord and what He could do through them. The spies were sent by Moses to find out the city's strengths and weaknesses so that they could prepare to conquer it. They found that there were giants in the land, the towns were fenced, and the inhabitants were ferocious people. It was intimidating, and ten of the twelve spies didn't believe they could conquer it. Going back to their own army, they brought an 'evil report' [Numbers 13:32] to scare everyone else. They didn't want to go up to battle, so they focused only on the strengths of their enemies in the report. Two of the spies, however, Joshua and Caleb, were confident in the Lord's strength. They said that in spite of the giants, 'the Lord is with us: fear them not' [Numbers 14:9]. I love that mindset. In the end, Caleb and Joshua were the only ones allowed to inherit the land. Because of their 'evil report,' the other ten spies would never live in the land.

"Forty-five years passed, and the ten spies who wouldn't believe all died from a plague. Caleb said, in Joshua 14 (and I love this), 'Forty years old was I when Moses . . . sent me . . . and I brought him word again as it was in mine heart. Nevertheless my brethren that went up with me made the heart of the people melt: but I wholly followed the Lord my God. And Moses sware on that day, saying, Surely, the land . . . shall be thine inheritance' [Joshua 14:7–9]. Verse 10 reads, 'And now, behold, the Lord hath kept me alive, as he said, these forty and five years.' So he was eighty-five! And then verse 11: 'As yet I am as strong this day as I was in the day that Moses sent me: as my strength was then, even so is my strength now, for war.' Finally, verse 12: 'Now therefore give me this mountain . . . for thou heardest in that day how the Anakims were there, and that the cities were great and fenced: if so be the Lord will be with me, then I shall be able to drive them out, as the Lord said.'

"So my brother sent that story to me, and then asked me in his letter: 'Who do you want to be as a missionary? Do you want to be one of the ten or one of the two? Do you want to see a challenge, get scared, and look for a way out? Or do you want to be the courageous type, put your confidence in the Lord, and see it through to the end?' It takes a special kind of confidence to say, 'God is with me; we're going to finish this.'"

Paul explained that he and his brothers in Christ "rejoice in Christ Jesus, and have no confidence in the flesh" (Philippians 3:3).

The more I talked with Bryan, the more I could see that he was like Ammon, Paul, and Caleb—his confidence was not "in the flesh." It came from his closeness to the scriptures and his relationship with Christ.

Bryan returned to BYU in July of 2005, having faithfully finished his mission. It's really no secret what a great football player Bryan Kehl became after. He came back and dominated as our defensive captain. I'll include only a summary of his stats: In his four years at BYU, he totaled 205 tackles. Bryan's senior year, he made the Mountain West all-conference team with 84 tackles, 4 sacks, 3 interceptions, and a touchdown. He had a tremendous game against New Mexico, accruing 10 tackles, an interception, a forced fumble, and a fumble recovery to boost the team to a 31–24 win; he was named the Mountain West Defensive Player of the Week for that performance. The Cougar defense he captained was ranked tenth in the nation, and Bryan was voted MVP of that defense by his teammates.

With such an excellent career, he caught the eyes of the New York Giants. They snatched Bryan up in the 2008 NFL Draft.

Bryan's confidence was certainly an important factor in his football success. Perhaps less known, however, was how much his confidence came into play when he sought to win the heart of the girl of his dreams. During all this time playing football, he was determined to catch the eye of Jessica Bingham.

Jessica: "My dad is a really good man. When I was looking for a spouse, I was looking for someone like my dad, and that's what helped me find Bryan. Bryan's been a huge blessing in my life. Not that he needs to hear that—he already knows it. But we get along really well. We have a lot of similarities. He was the only person I dated that I completely understood. Even now, he might say something no one else understands, but I totally get it. I always know what he's thinking. I think that attracted me to him. I just felt like we were on the same page."

Bryan: "I first saw her on campus right after my mission in the fall of 2005. I saw her walking on campus and she caught my eye, so I asked people who she was. Nate Meikle was the social butterfly, and somehow I knew Nate would know her. I asked him, and he told me she had a boyfriend but that they were on a break. So he gave me her number.

I called her out of the blue; I'd never talked to her before that, but I asked her out. She said no. 'I have a boyfriend. You don't really go out with other people when you have a boyfriend.' I said, 'Oh. Well, yeah, I talked to Nate, and he said you guys were on a break, but that's cool.' I smoothed it over. I even added, 'Well, when that doesn't work out, we'll go out then.' She said, 'Okay, sounds good.'

Jessica: "I didn't! I didn't say, 'Okay, I'll break up with my boyfriend, and then I'll call you!'"

Bryan: "Well, that is what she said."

Jessica: "For the record, I did *not* say, 'All right, sweet! I'll call you later.'"

Bryan: "Maybe she didn't say that exactly, but she did make it clear that she was ready to go out . . ."

Jessica (laughing): "That is so not true."

Bryan: "Even after that call, I would always talk to her whenever I saw her on campus."

Jessica: "Later on, when I found out who he was, I was like, 'Oh, he's cute. That's who I said no to?'"

Bryan: "I tried a second time in the spring of 2006, and even though she said no again, she made it fairly clear that she was ready to go out whenever."

Jessica: "Oh my gosh!"

Bryan: "So finally, I asked her out the third time in December of 2007. We went out and had a great time; it was fun. We went out three or four times in December, and then on January 1, I left. I went to go train for the NFL combine. We weren't even officially a dating couple when I proposed. We had never once talked about marriage. I got on the phone and called her parents to set it up. The idea occurred to me and it felt right, so I called them. I remember thinking, *Okay, I guess I'm gonna do this*, as I called them."

Jessica: "My mom was like, 'Is she going to say yes?'"

Bryan: "I said, 'Yeah!' I hadn't even thought about the possibility of her saying no until her mom asked me that. I look back at it now. Wow, I was crazy. But when I was planning it, I didn't think twice. The only thought on my mind was, *She'll say yes, and it'll be great*."

Jessica: "Tell how you proposed to me."

Bryan: "I was in New York with the Giants and I flew out to Salt Lake, so I surprised her. I took her in the car, and we went out to the airport where charter jets fly out. I had lined up a jet, so we got on this little private jet and flew around Ogden, Provo, and then the Salt Lake Temple. I got down, showed her the ring, and said, 'Will you marry me in that temple?' She asked, 'Are you serious?' We had never talked about marriage before."

Jessica: "The whole time, I had been thinking, *This is a really nice date. Maybe we'll be boyfriend and girlfriend now!*

Bryan: "I couldn't have drawn it up any better."

Jessica: "I've heard other girls say, 'I was so surprised when my husband proposed. We weren't even sure when the ring was going to be ready,' and I say to myself, 'They don't even know what a surprise is.'"

Bryan's confidence obviously helped him win his sweetheart over. Sweeping her off her feet, Bryan and Jessica were married in the Salt Lake Temple on July 22, 2009, after Bryan's rookie year in the NFL. In the meantime, Bryan employed that confidence into everything else he did. He had already become a starter for the Giants. I asked Bryan why he believed the Lord blessed him with so much athletic success.

Bryan: "'Many are called, but few are chosen' [D&C 121:34]. The Lord has blessed many people with athletic ability, and He's blessed everyone with great potential. So, many are called to be something great, but few are chosen because few actually make the choice themselves; few choose to cultivate their talents and see their full potential blossom, and even fewer choose to use their talents to bless other people. The Lord has blessed me, but I'm not unique in that way. The 'call' is issued to many people; it's just a matter of whether you answer it. In my mind, the way you answer is by being the kind of person kids can look up to. Unfortunately, in college sports, and even more in professional sports, the majority of gifted athletes don't do that.

"Another phrase that comes to mind: 'Where much is given, much is required' [D&C 82:3]. If you're blessed with athleticism, what are you going to do with it? So many athletes love the party in the great and spacious building. I try to be a standard, a light that kids can watch and say, 'Look at that guy from BYU. He keeps his standards.' There's so much more I should do, but I try.

"I believe that the Lord intended me to develop my talents as much as possible. He intends that for all of us. I always wanted to go to the NFL. I believed that a part of my patriarchal blessing pointed me in that direction. Knowing that patriarchal blessings are sacred, I'll share only a short quote: 'Your formal mission is for two years, Bryan, but your mission is for life. You were foreordained to teach the gospel, by example, to thousands of people. They will hear your testimony and understand the way.'

"During my mission, I remember thinking, *I'm working hard up here, but I'm not talking to thousands of people.* But my mission prepared me. When I got back home, I decided to never turn down an invitation to speak (as long as I didn't have some other commitment). I've now spoken at over 120 firesides—sometimes to groups as small as ten or so, and some over five hundred. I've literally testified to thousands of people, and I'm nowhere near being done. I truly feel that if I live a certain way, I can do things in the NFL that I couldn't do otherwise. And kids who are in desperate need, who might not listen to someone else, just might listen to me.

"Keeping your standards in the NFL can be tough. If I wanted to live a riotous life, it would be easy in the NFL; that gate is wide open. You have to watch yourself carefully, because little things other players do can rub off. I've watched others who I know are members of the Church, and little things like dirty language rub off on them. You're around filthy language all day long. You have to screen that out so you don't talk or think like everybody else.

"Personally, I don't think I do anything great or spectacular; I just consistently do little things. I try to be proactive and keep my spiritual reservoirs high. Before I was married, I went out with the missionaries on Tuesdays and Thursdays for a couple of hours in the evening. I still go out with the elders as often as I can, and my wife and I try to go to the temple every Friday. Little things like that keep our reservoirs high.

"I get asked all the time, 'What is playing in the NFL like?' In fact, that is probably the most commonly asked question of my football career. I always point out how fun the actual football in the NFL is, with the practices, the games, the competition being the best of the best. I absolutely love everything that happens between the sidelines. But then I always point out how much I don't like everything outside the sidelines: the business of the NFL. It truly is a business, and I've often said they treat us more like champion racehorses than appreciated employees.

"And this is probably why I miss playing at BYU so much. In college, it's still just a game (at least in most programs). The thing I miss most about BYU is the people—the other players and the coaches. One of my favorite things to do was relax in the locker room before meetings and after practice. You could go in there most any time of the day, and guys would be in there goofing off, hanging out, or whatever. In the NFL, when work is over, I can't wait to beeline for my car and head home. Most of the guys have completely different interests and standards than me, so I have no interest in spending much time with them. But at BYU, most all the guys had the same life goals and morals, and most were returned missionaries, so hanging out with them in the locker room is honestly one of the things I miss most about being there."

"Sometimes in the NFL, you have to be willing to be on your own. I'm not super tight with most of the guys. They're my friends, but I don't go and hang out with them. There are only a handful of guys I'm close to from the NFL, so that brotherhood I had at BYU is completely different now. But there are some solid Christian guys in the NFL. I definitely gravitate toward them.

"One good thing is that the other players never try to get me to do what they do. They respect my standards. They're not going to follow those standards themselves, but they're kind of impressed by them. Before I was married, I remember being asked often, 'You're a virgin? Really? No . . .' They were surprised but impressed. I've never had one person make fun of me for that."

In Lehi's vision of the tree of life, he saw many who entered a building that represented the world's vanity. "And great was the multitude that did enter into that strange building" (1 Nephi 8:33). Bryan's environment heavily involves that building. No one expects him to keep his standards, yet he "continually hold[s] fast to the rod of iron" (verse 30).

Athletically, he has done quite well. He's amassed 122 tackles (thus far) in his NFL career, with a sack, a deflected pass, and an interception. He made his first NFL start on October 26, 2008, against the Pittsburg

Steelers, picking off one of Ben Roethlisberger's passes and returning it for seventeen yards. Becoming so successful might be reason to celebrate, "eat, drink, and be merry," for some (2 Nephi 28:7). Instead, Bryan is continually concerned with his "spiritual reservoirs," as he called them. He proselytes with missionaries and visits the temple on weekends. While the worldly success he's attained in the NFL seems so glamorous, he maintains focus on "a treasure in the heavens that faileth not" (Luke 12:33). Where does such dedication come from?

Bryan: "There's a Church video I really like. It's corny, old-school, probably from the 1980s, but it's awesome. It's called *What Is Real?*[1] It uses the analogy of real life verses a play, and it shows that the point of scenery used onstage is to make the play look real. It shows that the whole question of life is, 'What is real?' Is the gospel real? Is God real? Is it just a made-up myth, or is it real? We all need to decide if there is a God. There are only two answers: He exists or He does not. There's no in-between. If the answer is yes, if you believe there is a God, the next questions are, 'What does He expect of me? Is He a God who doesn't care what I do? Is He a God who wants me to 'eat, drink and be merry' [2 Nephi 28:7—see previous], or is He a God who expects something?'

"You have to make that decision. If there is a God, if the Bible and the Book of Mormon are true, if the teachings of Jesus Christ are true, then whether you live the gospel alters your existence for eternity. If that's the case, it's important that you go to church, get baptized and receive the Holy Ghost, advance in the priesthood, keep your covenants, and get endowed in the temple. Most of all, it's important that you get married in the temple. It's not only important—it's life-threatening. Eternal life-threatening.

"If there is no God, or if He doesn't care what you do, then go ahead: eat, drink, and be merry; live a riotous life; do whatever you want. There's no gray ground, there's no in-between. It's either the one or the other. You have to decide. With the gospel, it's all-in; it's not 'I'm a Mormon on Sundays, and after that I'm just chilling.' No, you need to make a decision, and once you make a choice, live up to your choice. We've been taught the standards of the Church since we were CTRs and Sunbeams, so we know what to do. If it is true, if it is real, then all this does matter, and you need to follow it. That's really what it comes down to.

"If you do decide that this is real, that the gospel is worth fighting for, it may not seem as easy at first as the alternative. But if this is real, it's worth the fight. I love Elder Holland. He thinks the way I think. He totally speaks to me. One of his talks that really inspires me is called "However Long and Hard the Road." He says that life is tough, but you just persevere; you push forward. Sometimes, it looks like you're not going to make it, but you keep going. He says that sometimes you might have to lean on your sword and rest a while, and then rise and fight again. [Ether 15:29]. I love that comment because I think that's life—it's a battle. Sometimes, you faint because of the loss of blood, but you get up and you fight again. People need to realize that life is supposed to be hard and challenging. You're supposed to get tired. Sometimes, you might have to stop and rest momentarily, but the idea is to get up and fight again."

Since the time of our interview, and in the process of making drafts for this chapter, I asked Bryan to give me an update on how things were going in the NFL and with family life. He sent me an email in response, which included the following:

Bryan: "I tore my ACL running down the field, covering a punt at Dallas in October of my sixth NFL season. I fell down and knew something had happened to my knee, but I had no idea I had just torn 'the dreaded ACL.' I got up and walked off the field. I almost went back in too before I decided I had better go talk to the trainer first. I've played football since I was eight years old, and that was the first time I ever came out of a game because of an injury. I had reconstructive knee surgery on October 24 and have been rehabbing like crazy ever since. My last contract expired in March, so I'm now a free agent. Because I'm about to turn thirty and am coming off major knee surgery, my prospects are sadly slim. I don't know if I will ever play football again. Getting that opportunity is out of my hands—it's up to the NFL scouts. I told my agent, 'When I get that chance, I'm going to be ready.' I will make the coaches and scouts who see me work out say, 'Wow, this guy tore his ACL? You would never know.' My goal is to be bigger, faster, and stronger than I've ever been. I am on pace. If they give me the chance, I will play for many more years. But if it isn't in the cards, if that isn't what the Lord has in store for me, I will gladly 'go where You want me to go, dear Lord' [*Hymns*, 270].

"Jayda is twenty-one months old and the joy of our life. I am biased, of course, but I think she might just be the strongest and smartest two-year-old baby out there. She is a wonder child. Jessica just gave birth to our baby boy, Cruz, five days ago. [This email was sent May 15, 2014]. He was nine pounds, seven ounces, and he looks to be headed right down the same path of greatness his big sister has blazed ahead. My wife is a champ and is bouncing right back from pregnancy and labor as fast as ever. She truly is the love of my life.

"On Saturday morning, I was holding my little boy, seven hours old, and my little girl came running in to see him for the first time. She hopped up on my lap too, and for the first time, I held both my kids together and looked at my sweet wife as she took a picture. It may have been the best moment of my life."

Notes

1. YouTube "LDS Film—What Is Real?" to see the video.

ANDREW GEORGE

"Stand ye in holy places, and be not moved" (D&C 87:8).

*M*y interview with Andrew George left an old child-hood memory replaying in my mind. I remember my father showing me a flock of ducks when I was little. *"How do the ducks fly, Brock?"* he asked. *Being only six or seven years old, I was anxious to please Dad, so I shouted out the first obser-vation I could make: "Together!"*

"That's right!" Dad said. He showed me a little Polaroid he had of an eagle, wings outstretched, with nothing in the background but the sky. "And how does an eagle fly, buddy?"

"Alone!" I quickly responded.

"That's right, son." Dad then began to relate this to my life. "The older you get, the more your friends around you may make wrong choices. Sometimes they're like ducks; they only make those decisions because they're following their friends. They follow the popular kids, whether those popular kids are wrong or right. But you're not like them, son. You're not a duck. You're an eagle, and you can show your friends how to be eagles. Show them that it doesn't matter what the rest of the crowd does. The only thing that matters is doing what's right. You have to be brave enough to soar alone. Sometimes you'll be alone; sometimes

people will tease you, but when your true friends see you, they'll want fly away from the crowd, like you."

Even though I was barely old enough to understand the metaphor, my dad's words sunk deep into my heart. I was filled with determination to set my own course and not to allow "the crowd" to alter my destiny. My father's simple lesson stuck with me and played a huge part in all my decisions throughout high school and college. To this day, I teach the same metaphor in seminary classes.

Andrew and his wife, Tawny, talked with me in their home in Provo. They both grew up amongst peers who were mostly not LDS, and they told me about decisions they made that separated them from the crowd. That childhood memory instantly came back to mind. They're eagles, I kept thinking to myself. More than anything else, the warrior-like trait I noticed in them was their ability to "fly" a separate way than the crowd did, especially during high school. They often soared alone. I had played with Andrew and had noticed him leave the other football stars he played with from time to time, and take time to encourage walk-ons and those who struggled for playing time, like me. I had already seen that Andrew was an eagle because of his actions.

The Georges have a down-to-earth feeling to them. I often forgot, during the course of the interview, that I was talking with a BYU football star. It seemed Andrew had forgotten that as well. He and Tawny were friendly, chatting with me for a while about their kids before we started the interview. I could tell they really adored their kids. They laughed as they told me their two-year-old son, Jack, had just requested "Cheetos and blue drink" (Powerade) for dinner.

After we laughed and talked about our kids, I started working my way into some of the interview questions. This is where it became clear that both Andrew and Tawny had become eagles in their earlier years. Both possessed warrior spirits. It was also clear that Andrew had been a warrior not only in football. I asked him when he first started developing a desire to choose the right.

Andrew: "I remember one of my best friends when I was in elementary school. He was a kid who didn't have a lot of parental involvement. His family had a lot of money, though. They had a really cool house with a pool, and I loved to go over there and hang out with them. But my parents saw early on that no one was watching us. They also saw some of the things that his older sister got involved in, and they started to worry about my friendship. I remember them asking me not to go to his house when his parents weren't around. I thought, *Why? He's so fun!*

"We don't always see what our parents see. I didn't see what my parents saw. If I could tell young people what I've learned from experience, I'd say trust those around you. It could be your parents, a religious leader, or a brother or sister—they will have a different perspective than you have. Listen to their advice. Ultimately, you have to make your own decisions, but there are people who will guide you and help you choose the right friends. Stick with gospel principles. Choose good friends who are in alignment with what you believe. There are people around you who absolutely get what you're going through, even if you think otherwise."

Tawny: "And they love you too. When you're young, you think your parents just want to make your life miserable, that they don't want you to have friends or be cool. But they love you and want what's best for you."

Andrew: "I slowly started to veer away from that friend. He got into drinking and drugs, so I started making different friends. I made a lot of different friends along the way, but the best person I ever made friends with was Mick Lindquist. He lived right behind me, and we did absolutely everything together. He and I are still best friends to this day; he's the one friend who has remained constant for the last twenty years. Others have come and gone, but I really made one friend who carried me through high school. He stayed true to his Christian standards and helped me make good decisions."

Tawny: "Even though he wasn't LDS, I think he respected you for your religion."

Andrew: "He knew what I believed in. He would even push me to be better because he knew the standards I needed to be keeping. He never drank or did drugs or anything like that. He was just a good guy who had a great sense of humor and loved to go out and have fun."

Tawny: "I think having someone like that, who will hold you to your standards, helps you want to be better."

Andrew: "Could be a parent, your priests quorum or Laurel advisor, or a really good friend."

Tawny: "Just someone to turn to. Much of the time, people who get lost in high school don't have that. If they have bad friends, or if their parents aren't there, they don't have anyone to motivate them."

Andrew: "My group of friends in high school really shaped me. I grew up in Denver and went to a large high school. There were thirty-six, thirty-seven hundred kids, but not many were LDS—I would say about 2 percent of the student population. In that respect, I was definitely the minority, but people knew that I was LDS. Everyone knew who the LDS kids at the high school were. So that's what a lot of people associated with me; I was a Mormon kid. I took pride in that, and I didn't want to let anybody down. I wasn't going to make anyone question my religion.

"I tried to do things that would reflect positively on the Church. I was fortunate to have a group of friends who were really good guys. They weren't LDS, but they weren't into the party scene. They weren't into the drugs or any of those other things that were going on. On top of that, we were all athletes, so we were all pushing each other in that respect too. We set a standard for each other on how hard we should work. That shaped my work ethic, going into BYU."

Tawny: "A good sign to look for when you're choosing friends is how involved they are. Andrew said he had that connection with his friends—they all played sports together. They all had a common goal, working together. It could be music for some students, student government for others. Having a passion for something, I believe, keeps them out of trouble."

Andrew: "It's just like the gospel: one thing that keeps people in the Church is having a calling because that gives them something to be involved in. A lot of the kids I knew in high school were doing bad things because they didn't have anything to do after school. That's a generality, but the kids making good decisions were involved in extracurricular things. It could be athletics, student government, chess club, whatever. It doesn't matter what it is; as long as it's something good and keeps you busy, and you enjoy it, then it'll help you stay out of trouble."

Tawny: "There were probably even fewer members of the Church in my school. [Tawny went to Northglenn High School in Thornton, Colorado—about forty minutes away from Andrew's high school in

Denver.] I was lucky enough to have friends who stayed out of trouble for the most part, until our senior year. During freshman, sophomore, and junior years, they were like me: involved in sports. Senior year, they started having boyfriends and doing things I didn't want to be involved in. I steered away at that point.

"Some decisions you make affect the rest of your life. It sounds cliché, but making the decision to stay moral and obey the Word of Wisdom was a huge crossroads point for me. I got to BYU because of high school decisions about morality and the Word of Wisdom. I decided on the type of young man I wanted to date and ultimately marry because of those same things.

"When I think about warriors, I think of Nephi saying, 'I will go and do the things which the Lord hath commanded' [1 Nephi 3:7]. We're taught the things we're supposed to do; we know what's right and wrong. In high school, it can feel like we're blindly doing the right things. It may seem like, 'Why waste the time?' But if you 'go and do' the things you're supposed to do, you'll be blessed, and those little decisions will end up making a huge difference in your life."

Andrew: "I'm like Tawny. Small decisions led to bigger decisions that affected me all the way up to now, and they will probably continue to do so in the future. One big decision happened when I met Tawny; deciding to marry her was big! But what set me up for that was the decision to serve a mission, and that decision was set up by my senior year in high school. I remember that the end of my senior year, everyone was planning this senior campout. All the seniors were going to meet at a campsite, get drunk, and worse things would follow. I remember thinking, *I will not be a part of this. This is not important. This is not what I want to be around. I need to make sure I'm on the right path to serve a mission.* I was less than a year away. Right then, I made the decision: *I need to be ready, when the time comes, to serve a mission.* Being a part of those social groups wasn't important."

As Andrew and Tawny shared these experiences from their teenage years, the thought crossed my mind, Little decisions like these, to do what's right, have affected more than just their own lives. People will read their stories and desire to be "eagles" themselves. Why? Because two high school kids in Colorado kept their standards.

"By small and simple means are great things brought to pass" (Alma 37:6), and small decisions during high school can affect many, many people, just as Andrew's and Tawny's have.

Andrew was an outstanding football player in high school. As a first-team All-State tight end, he averaged twenty-three yards per catch. He was recruited by Wyoming, Oregon, Stanford, Air Force, and Utah, but he chose to accept a scholarship to BYU after serving his mission.

Andrew: "I served in the England London South Mission from 2003 to 2005. This, of course, is the best mission in the world. One thing I loved about my mission was the melting pot of cultures I was exposed to. I taught and interacted with people from England, Africa, Asia, Europe, and the Middle East—pretty much everywhere in the world. I also lived in a country with a rich history, and I was able to experience that on preparation days with visits to many historical sites and national parks. This was truly a unique experience that I think about daily.

"One of the most satisfying experiences from my mission came just over two years after it had ended, actually. I went back to visit with my wife and spent some time in Poole, one of the areas I had served in for quite some time. Upon attending church, I was reacquainted with several of the Church members there, whom I had grown to love and appreciate for their devotion to the gospel.

"I also saw a man named Mark Why attending church. When I had been serving in Poole, my companion and I began teaching Mark. His wife and kids were already members of the Church, but up to this point, Mark had not shown a lot of interest. As time went on, we developed a friendship with him, and he began to trust us to come over. I ended up leaving the area only a few weeks after we started teaching Mark. About five to six months later, I returned home, and Mark had still not joined the Church. That was the last I had heard until the day I showed up to that ward in Poole with Tawny, to learn that Mark had decided to get baptized and join the Church only a few months earlier. Mark pulled me aside at church, and we talked for quite a while about his decision to get baptized. He said that Elder Mulliss and I were the first ones to come around and really show a deep interest in him. He told me he would never forget his first missionaries who brought the gospel to him and changed his life forever.

"Previous to this, I hadn't known if Mark would ever join the Church. I didn't know if I had even had an impact on him. But two years later, to see him strong in the gospel and receiving great blessings from his membership in the Church, brought me so much joy! Elder Mulliss and I had worked hard to break down barriers with Mark. We spent many evenings planning the best way to reach him and how best to teach him important principles he was struggling with. To hear, from him, that we'd had an impact on his journey brought me personal satisfaction and validation for the work I had done years ago."

Andrew returned from the mission and worked out with the football team for a year and a half, redshirting in 2005. He met Tawny in the fall of 2006. They started dating seriously halfway through his freshman football season.

Andrew: "Tawny and I met in the fall of 2006. We both had previous relationships end, and we had a mutual friend, Brett Denney, who introduced us to each other. We had met before and kind of knew each other, but not well. Tawny grew up in the same ward as Brett, and he and I were teammates at the time. He didn't have to do much to get things started. Once he set us up on a date, everything progressed from there easily. Because we had both just gotten out of serious relationships, we knew what it felt like for things to be wrong. So when we started dating each other, it was refreshing and easy to tell that this was different. We both knew pretty quickly that this was right, and after dating for about six months, we were engaged. We were married about three months later, on June 30, in the Denver Colorado Temple."

In the years to come, Andrew became an incredibly successful football player. There were a few games that had special significance to him.

Andrew: "I don't think Heavenly Father cares at all about sports; He doesn't care about wins and losses. What He does care about are His children. The example in my head right now is the Oklahoma game in 2009. I sort of had a spiritual experience, feeling that we were going to win the game before it even started. I didn't tell anyone; I thought, *That's dumb, I don't want to tell people I know we're going to win this game; it's just football.* But after the game, I was bawling. It was the weirdest thing—I don't ever cry."

Tawny: "Nope."

Andrew (laughing): "I never cry. It's just not something that comes up easily in me. But at the end of this game, I was absolutely bawling. I was so embarrassed—I wouldn't take my helmet off. I remember Dennis Pitta looking at me and asking, 'Are you crying right now?' I just smiled and said, 'Yeah, I don't know why.'

"Again, Heavenly Father probably doesn't care about football. There are a lot of things that just don't matter. But He does care about our righteous desires. I had this feeling that He was aware of the things I wanted and the things I worked really hard for. That's more what it was about. It wasn't about the fact that we beat Oklahoma; it was just a feeling that He cared about me. Maybe others were inspired during the game by my playing ability, my leadership, or something like that. But it was probably even more for me—to learn how to be a leader through athletics. Through the work that I put into that game, the Lord taught me about teamwork, how to work well with others, and about humility and hard work. There's a lot you learn through athletics, but it gets lost in the shuffle if you only worry about wins and losses."

Andrew scored BYU's first touchdown to tie things up in the beginning of that 14–13 victory over number three Oklahoma. Andrew was never the star of the team, however. Fellow inside receiver Dennis Pitta, who would later score a touchdown for the Baltimore Ravens to help win Super Bowl XLVII, would get most of the media's attention throughout Andrew's career. This could have been cause for competition or jealousy, but Andrew saw things in a different light.

Tawny: "Even after his mission, Andrew was a great example of humility, especially in football. Dennis Pitta was one of his best friends. Since they played in the same position, their relationship could have been competitive, but they worked together and challenged each other."

Andrew: "We had a great relationship. We could have had a rivalry between us, but we spent a lot of time helping each other, critiquing.

We were both good players, but there were a lot of things Dennis did better than me. That just pushed me to try and do those things as well as him. He was always good to me. Why let competition affect our relationship? We spent our time pushing each other, trying to make each other better.

"I heard a quote: 'Stop worrying about what people have and start finding out who they are.' That's like my relationship with Dennis—we never compared the number of catches or plays, or what publicity we got. We were best friends.

"That's applicable to anyone, especially with high school students. They're in a tough environment and are constantly being compared to other people. High school is a materialistic setting. It's tough to get over someone making fun of you for what you're wearing, the way you talk, or the way you look. You have to learn to care less about what Joe on the other end of the hallway is saying and more about choosing the right."

Andrew worked hard, learning and improving with Dennis Pitta. Defenses worried too much about Pitta in 2009, and Andrew's quiet, consistent ability caught such defenses off guard. This led to Andrew's opening touchdown against Oklahoma, and he performed spectacularly against New Mexico that same year, the day his son Jack was born.

Andrew's quiet consistency would also prove lethal against Utah. In the last game of the regular season, the Cougars found themselves trailing Utah 23–20 in overtime. According to regulations, each team was granted one possession with an opportunity to score, and Utah's possession had resulted in a field goal. The Cougars would need to score during their possession. A touchdown would win them the game, a field goal would tie things up and send them into another round of overtime, and failure to score would result in Utah's win. On the second down and twenty-five yards from the end zone, sports commentators surmised that Utah's defense was overly focused on Pitta, who had just broken Austin Collie's record of 215 career catches. Andrew ran a perfect, unnoticed route and was left wide open for a quick dump pass. Andrew found nobody between him and the end zone, running in for an easy touchdown.[1]

Once again, Andrew's less-noticed consistency caught a defense off guard. The instant Andrew strode into the end zone for the win, his teammates piled on top of him in celebration, and screaming fans flooded the field. This was a perfect way to cap off his senior year.

Andrew finished his senior year with 30 catches, 408 yards, and 5 touchdowns. His career at BYU resulted in 70 catches, 827 yards, and 11 touchdowns. The highlight in most Cougar fans' memories was this thrilling overtime touchdown to beat Utah.

Andrew: "I have been able to learn what it's like to really fight for something through athletics. In the games against Utah and Oklahoma, I wanted to win so badly, so I played hard. Those games really brought out the fighting spirit in me. Football gave me the feeling of what it's like to really want something. It gave me the desire to really fight for such things. It helped me learn how to put all of my time and effort into achieving something. I learned what that feels like, and now I apply it to other parts of my life. I've applied it in academics and to my family. I try now to have that same passion in other aspects of my life, that same fighting spirit."

Tawny: "Usually, people look up to the guys who have had success all of the time. Sometimes, though, the role models are the players who were not great at first but worked hard and got better. They might not have had as much success in the beginning, but they worked their way up. Andrew isn't playing professional football right now, and he wasn't the star all through college, but people look up to him. He's served in our ward as a Young Men's leader, and the boys have looked up to him so much."

Andrew: "I wasn't too vocal a leader on the team, but I was someone who more than anything tried to lead by example. I wanted to set the standard by being at all the workouts and working hard in practices. As a starter on the team my junior and senior seasons, I wanted to set an example of how you were supposed to play games, how you were supposed to approach games, and how you were supposed to act on the team. It's nice to know that Coach Mendenhall recognized that. I'm surprised that he included me on that list of 'warriors,' because most of the time the only leaders who get noticed are the vocal ones. I definitely wasn't a vocal leader, so it's good to know that he noticed me just trying to lead by example.

"After my career at BYU, I wanted to try my hand in the NFL. Playing professionally had been a goal of mine for quite some time, and I was anxious to give it a shot. I trained hard in my preparation for the 2010 NFL Draft and was hopeful that I would be drafted in the later rounds. When the day came, I didn't end up getting drafted, but I did sign a free agent contract with the Carolina Panthers immediately following the draft. I spent the summer of 2010 in Charlotte, training with the team in the hopes that I could make their final roster. I ended up getting cut by the Panthers a couple weeks before their fall training camp.

"Though I was disappointed that things didn't work out, I was soon signed by the Buffalo Bills. I went through training camp with the Bills, played in two pre-season games, and was ultimately cut on the final day of camp, when they had to trim their roster from seventy-five players down to fifty-three. I stayed in shape for several months, hoping I would get another opportunity, but unfortunately nothing worked out. This was a frustrating and discouraging time for me, knowing that my NFL dream was cut short. Having played at that level, I knew I was good enough to play for someone, but I didn't find the right opportunity."

Andrew didn't let his outer circumstances determine the fight within; he knew football wasn't the only venue in which he could be a warrior. He moved on from the NFL to take a job in healthcare administration, and then came back to the Y as an assistant coach.

Tawny: "Sometimes when you think things aren't fair in life, you become bitter and angry, but Andrew never let it get that way. There were probably some frustrating moments with the NFL falling through, but he used that as motivation. There were other guys who were given different opportunities, and maybe he wasn't in the right place at the right time. But that never got him down. It moved him on to something else. Instead of hanging onto his football dreams, he knew the Lord was taking him a different direction."

Andrew: "Circumstances may change, but my life calling won't. I wasn't foreordained to play football. I was foreordained to be a priesthood holder and a father—that will never change.

"As much as I love playing football—I love the game, I love coaching, I love being a part of it—football doesn't matter. We're not going to be playing football in the celestial kingdom by any means. Many of the things in this world do not matter, but it's hard to keep that perspective when the world wants you to think they do matter. There's nothing wrong with football—I've learned a lot of good lessons from the game. It's fun, but it doesn't matter on the grand scale. I wasn't put on this earth to be a football player; I'm not anymore, and I've only lived a third of my life. So there are things that are important, and then there are things that are really important. True warriors are the ones fighting the spiritual battles.

"In Sunday School, we were talking about Abinadi and his influence on Alma. Abinadi was a true warrior, fighting a spiritual battle. What impressed me was Abinadi's attitude of never giving up. I don't think he even knew exactly whom he was trying to convert; he was speaking directly to the king, but Alma was the one watching. Even though Alma had fallen away from the gospel, even though he wasn't making great choices, he was touched. He decided to change his life. Abinadi didn't know that.

"So the conversion chain goes from Abinadi converting Alma the Elder to Alma the Elder converting Alma the Younger, his son. Alma the Younger shows the depth of his conversion when he said, 'O that I were an angel, and could have the wish of mine heart, that I might go forth and speak with the trump of God, with a voice to shake the earth, and cry repentance unto every people! Yea, I would declare unto every soul, as with the voice of thunder, repentance and the plan of redemption, that they should repent and come unto our God, that there might not be more sorrow upon all the face of the earth' [Alma 29:1–2]. Abinadi probably had no idea he was going to have this kind of effect.

"My favorite story is of Abinadi and his example. He did what he knew was right. The influence he had on future generations, without even knowing it, is really cool.

"Then Alma the Younger said [in verse 3], 'But behold, I am a man, and do sin in my wish; for I ought to be content with the things which the Lord hath allotted unto me.' I especially love this third verse, where he said he wanted to be more; he wasn't content with how far he'd come. As a person, he wanted even more, and I think that some-times it's the same thing with us; we maybe don't give thanks enough. We're not content with the great things the Lord has blessed us with. We want more, we want to be like someone else, or we want the things that someone else has. We've got to be content with the things the Lord has given us. I'm so grateful for the time Heavenly Father did give me with football, but I'm also grateful for all the other opportunities He's given me after that.

"I graduated BYU with a degree in business finance, and that degree helped me get a job in healthcare; my experience as a collegiate and professional athlete helped me as well."

Tawny: "He became a healthcare administrator in California. It wasn't the most glamorous job. He was working in nursing homes and had to work on every level in those facilities—with the nurses' assistants, janitors, and maintenance people, training them on their jobs. Even on those levels, he would go in and give 100 percent, even when it might not have been the prettiest or most enjoyable job. I've noticed that in everything he does, from working in jobs like that to raising our son—he's giving it 100 percent."

Andrew: "In every venue I worked in, I always tried to remember one thing, which was being an administrator didn't make me any better than anyone else. Just because I was maybe more educated than some-one else or had a position that was more distinguished, that didn't make me better. The janitorial staff and the nurses' assistants are the people on the front line of work—it's not glamorous, and often they get pushed aside. But what they do is important work, and they're important people. They maybe just didn't have the same opportunities I had.

"After finishing as a healthcare administrator, I had the itch to coach at the college level. I wanted to see if there would be an oppor-tunity as a graduate assistant at BYU. I was brought in for an inter-view and hired about a week later. We moved back to Provo from California in March 2012 to start another adventure as a family. I was also accepted to the executive MBA program at BYU and began working on my master's degree while coaching on the football staff."

Andrew coached at BYU 2012–13. Since the interview, Andrew accepted a job with Merrill Lynch as a financial analyst and is enjoying this new opportunity. Andrew and Tawny just had their third child, Noah, on May 16, 2014.

Andrew: "Tawny is an outstanding mother, and I am grateful for the work she does in our home every day. Taking care of four-year-old Jack, one-year-old Madelyn, and newborn Noah keeps her plenty busy and is a tremendous accomplishment. We are blessed to have three healthy kids, a good job that supports our family, and the gospel of Jesus Christ in our home to provide direction and strength."

Notes

1. YouTube "Andrew George Max Hall 2009" for some exciting videos of Andrew's game-winning play.

SHAUN NUA

"Pray always, that you may come off conqueror" (D&C 10:5).

I scheduled my interview with Shaun Nua at BYU's student athlete building. We talked shortly before Shaun's flight out to the East Coast, where he would begin football camp. He coaches defensive line at the Naval Academy.

Shaun's senior year was in 2004, so I never met him before our interview. Of the ten players I interviewed, Shaun's physical frame was the most intimidating. Shaun is six-feet five-inches tall and 270 pounds. He played in the NFL and won a Super Bowl ring, and his muscular composition affirmed that he was an extraordinary athlete.

What surprised me more than his physical stature was how calm I became as soon as he started speaking with me. There was a peace in his voice I hadn't sensed over the phone. It was contagious—when he spoke, I felt calm. With each question, he would pause and take a deep breath before his response. I sensed that he was real and sincere, in no rush to impress me with his responses—just confident that the Spirit could help him say what future readers most needed to hear. While the world associates the word warrior *with violence, I felt a true warrior-like strength in Shaun's peaceful nature. His peace exuded confidence. Throughout the interview, I asked questions about the latter-day warrior in him. Where had he learned such peaceful strength?*

Shaun: "I grew up in Pago Pago, Samoa. When I was a kid, my dad was not the nicest guy. Back then, I thought it was just Polynesian discipline—a Samoan dad disciplining his kid. But looking back on it, it was so bad that I hated the guy. I never felt accepted by him. He made me feel like I was never going to be good enough. For some reason, I always remember praying. Maybe it wasn't full-on prayer, but I always talked to God. I would say things like, 'Please, God, don't let him beat me up too bad today,' or, 'God, please don't let him make his flight home today.' I realize now that those were superficial prayers, but I believed in expressing my desires to a higher power. I really couldn't go to my best friend and say, 'Please, stop my dad.' No one else was going to stop him. I just remember praying, and that habit has stayed with me.

"For a long time, there was a lot of anger inside because of my childhood. I started playing football my freshman year in high school, and football was probably where I unleashed most of my anger. It was such a good way to vent frustrations; I loved it so much. Ever since I began playing, football was on my mind. Even though I was on an island where only two or so families had a TV, I snuck out, found those TVs, and watched the games."

Shaun's love for football continued to be a way that he channeled his anger. Shaun won all-league honors as a defensive end in high school. Shaun had fight in him and great potential, but he mentioned that during the teenage years, he became a little prideful. An injury his senior year, however, caused Shaun to remember his childhood habit of prayer. Because Shaun was continually "com[ing] unto [the Lord]" through prayer, the Lord was able to "show unto [him his] weakness," or his pride. The Lord was able to "make weak things become strong" (Ether 12:27), and one of Shaun's greatest strengths is now humility.

Shaun: "Humility is how He molded me. Before He humbled me, I *knew* I was a bad dude. I could play basketball, football, and volleyball. I was blessed with so much athleticism, but I got a little arrogant. I started talking back to my mom. I knew I would get a scholarship to whatever school I wanted; I was going to be 'the man,' and everything was going to be run through me. Then I injured my knee right before my senior year in high school. Suddenly, I couldn't do anything, and I couldn't play football my senior year.

"I finally sat back and realized how quickly something could be taken away. That's how He humbled me; I will never forget that feeling. I believe that's how He helped me channel and focus my energy, that warrior-like mentality. Sooner or later, you have to be humble, or every-thing will be taken from you. I learned to be grateful and show gratitude for the things I had taken for granted. It helped with my overconfident attitude. If you're grateful, you realize that there's a reason you've been given power, and that reason is not self-glory.

"Dick LeBeau has been the defensive coordinator for the Pittsburg Steelers for years. That defense always dominates, but the guy never gives himself credit. You meet him and you'd think he didn't know anything about defense. He's so humble and grateful for everything. If you listen to any interview, he always credits his players. If the players pin him to the point where he can't credit them, he credits good luck. That's my point: When you feel like you have power or abilities, try your best not to take it in. Try your best not to say, 'Yeah, that was all me.' Make something good out of it. Help somebody else. Help an underconfident player. Give glory to God, where it all comes from. I had a hard time with that at first.

"When I injured my knee, there was nothing the doctor could have said to comfort me. There was nothing my mom or dad could have said either. Prayer was the only thing that comforted me when I was injured, and that brought me humility. I remember saying, 'Sorry, Lord, for getting too prideful.' Somehow, a comfort came out of that, the only comfort I really had. My dad was no comfort. My mom was always a sweet lady; she just let things go. My grandparents didn't even know what football was, so they were just like, 'You'll be fine.' Nothing any of them could have said would've comforted me as much as prayer did."

Through prayer, Shaun regained humility, and with time he regained strength in his knee. As his knee recovered, athletic ability started coming back. Shaun began dominating street basketball games in his neighborhood. Football was always in the back of his mind, but continuing with football would mean leaving the basketball games. He would have to leave the island and be a walk-on at a college in the United States.

Shaun: "There's a park next to our home called Lion Park. I would go and play basketball with a big group of kids every afternoon around six. The games were battles. I think about the kids from my childhood. They looked up to the older guys that stayed home and dominated the backyard basketball court. I admired them too. Part of me wanted to stay home and be like them.

"On the other hand, I knew that if I stayed home my whole life, it was going to be a dead end. It was going to be hard leaving my friends and my sisters and brother, but I knew there was something greater out there for me. There was something beyond our island, something beyond the kids at that park. I loved them, but I could sense that it wasn't for me. I felt like I wouldn't have a real relationship with my dad unless I was successful, and I didn't even feel like Division 1 football was going to be enough. I was determined to make that dude happy. I wanted to play in the NFL. You have to believe in that kind of stuff; you don't have to go out and be Michael Jordan, but you have to want to achieve more than what's handed to you on a platter.

"My whole family is religious. We are strong non-denominational Christians. Even after my injury, my older sister, for some reason, still believed that I could play football. She always had a feeling I needed to come with her to the States. She felt that was the best place for me to grow and mature spiritually. I remember getting phone calls from her back when I was in high school. She would tell me how she felt, and I used to say, 'Yes, I want to come to the States with you.' (She was at Arizona State at the time.) But my parents did not see it that way. It looked like my chances with football were done, and their attitude was, 'Now you're going to stay here and help the family out. Stay and work on the plantation for the family.'

"Youth who are fighters inside, if they're like me, will be tempted to argue a lot with their parents. They have to develop humility and patience. They can't see the bigger picture if they're caught up in family disagreements. They will think they know what's right. I'm speaking from experience, because I always thought I did, and I'd fight anybody for what I thought was right. Dad would tell me college wasn't the right thing to do, and I wanted to prove to him, right then, that he was wrong. But since then, I've learned that's not always the right thing to do. A better way is to have patience, if you're humble enough. Sit back and wait for the bigger picture to unfold. You don't have to make everybody see it right away. Be patient, be humble.

"Somehow, my sister ended up convincing my parents that if I stayed home, nothing good was going to happen. She convinced them I needed to go to college. I asked her, 'How did you persuade them?' I didn't even get a B in high school. She could tell I was a bit of a troublemaker, so I guess she told my parents, 'If he stays there, he's just going to get drunk every night and do no good for himself.'

"She played a big role in getting me to college. But looking back, God did it—His way to my parents was through my sister. Without her, there was no way they were going to budge.

"They had always said, 'He hurt his knee, and he's not a smart student. Shaun's calling is to help out at the house with the family.' But my sister somehow found a way to convince them to send me up to Arizona after my senior year.

"So I graduated from high school and went to Arizona with no plan. I missed that first football season trying to get my knee back to full strength. Then I went to walk-on to a couple of junior colleges—Mesa, Phoenix—but coaches were doubtful because of my injury. Eventually, an LDS coach at Eastern Arizona Community College named Scott Giles called. He was the only one who gave me a shot, and I went to play football at Eastern Arizona."

"GOD HATH CHOSEN THE FOOLISH THINGS OF THE WORLD
TO CONFOUND THE WISE; AND GOD HATH CHOSEN
THE WEAK THINGS OF THE WORLD TO CONFOUND THE
THINGS WHICH ARE MIGHTY" (1 CORINTHIANS 1:27).

Shaun: "I love underdogs. I'll always be an underdog. If I watch a game and an underdog is playing, I cheer for him. I find the story within it and always go with the underdogs. Why? Because I was one. Nothing was promising in the beginning. Nothing. Coach Giles invited me to come play, but there was no scholarship. I had to walk-on with a bum knee. I was determined to make my dad proud, though, so I worked like crazy.

"People have to take a chance with you. Coach Giles—I will never forget that man—gave me everything by taking a chance on me. I knew that was my chance. That's what you call an opportunity, and you have to take advantage. Underdogs don't have a lot of opportunities, so they have to be grateful for the few chances that come. A kid who comes from humble circumstances may only get one chance at something better. If he misses the boat, he goes back to whatever tough situation he started in. I knew that was my chance, and I don't think I ever missed a practice or a class.

"It was hard—I was a college-age kid, and sometimes partying or hanging out seemed more exciting than staying home and studying. But I knew this was my opportunity. Staying focused taught me so much about toughness—kids think toughness is being able to beat somebody up or drinking and showing everybody you can have a good time. But I think toughness is choosing to walk away, and maybe even be bored on a party night because you're studying. To me, being tough is being that kid who's strong enough to say, 'I don't want to go out tonight.' Real toughness is being able to say no."

At Eastern Arizona, Shaun became an All-American defensive end. That was eventually how he caught the attention of BYU recruiters. Shaun was offered a full scholarship and came to play as a Cougar.

Shaun: "Every time I see Coach Giles, I can see that he is happy he took that chance on me. I look back on that opportunity I had, and I think I took full advantage of it. Without that, I wouldn't feel like I could influence any of the kids back home. I would just be some guy working at the plantation, with no confidence in his ability to influence people. Now I feel like I have that power. If I didn't take that opportunity, I wouldn't be in this position to inspire others.

"So I started playing at the Y my junior year. While I was there as a player, my faith was still based on my religion back home. My family had helped me spiritually; my grandpa was quite spiritual. He prayed for everything—he prayed for his crops to grow, even for his pigs to be fat.

"I had learned to pray like him, so I never missed praying before a game, but the funny thing is I didn't pray after a lot of games. Those prayers did help me; there are so many challenges in football, and I do believe the Lord helped me through those challenges when I asked Him. But at the same time, I wasn't remembering to show gratitude after the games. I guess I was always praying for results. I prayed to win.

"Since then, I've learned to pray for the strength to handle any result. Now, when I go into a game, I don't pray to win; I pray that whatever the outcome is, I can handle it well. And I remember gratitude more now—gratitude for any outcome, whether I want it or not. That habit of prayer keeps getting stronger, and I find myself praying more and more often.

"I played really well my junior year, but the fall before my senior year, Bronco put me on the fourth team. I think he saw areas where my attitude could improve, and he wanted me to work my way back into the starting rotation. I changed my attitude, worked hard, and ended up making it as a starter for the whole season. There were a lot of good players on our defensive line. There was John Denney, who's playing in the NFL right now, and Manaia Brown, who's a straight-up beast, and Vince Feula. There were a lot of good players on the D-line with me. But one of my happiest moments in football was when I won the Defensive Lineman of the Year Award my senior year.

In BYU's defensive scheme, linemen are generally assigned to sustain blocks, and linebackers are freed up to make the majority of the tackles. Despite that, Shaun racked up fifty-four tackles and ten sacks for a combined loss of seventy-two yards, and sixteen tackles behind the line of scrimmage for a total loss of ninety-four yards in the two years he played at the Y. NFL scouts recognized Shaun's talent, and Shaun was drafted by the Pittsburg Steelers in 2005. With the Steelers, he won a Super Bowl ring in 2006.

Shaun: "All of the stuff I went through with my dad was probably what made me so determined to do this. I mean, my love for football was strong, so I wanted to do this for myself too. But my dad was always in the back of my head. I never told anybody along the way, but I think he got me to where I'm at now. I'm not saying that's the way it should be. That's not the way I'm going to do it; I think there is a better way, but I'm happy it worked out for me. It made me look at life a little different.

"Right now, my dad and I have the best relationship—the best! I love it. It probably took me getting drafted into the NFL to get him to accept me, and knowing that kept driving me. Everybody told me, 'You shouldn't credit him,' but for me, I forgive the dude. We have the best relationship now. I try to fly him out to games as much as I can."

Around this time, Shaun began investigating the Church. Improving his relationship with his dad definitely brought happiness, but Shaun started to see that winning a Super Bowl ring had only brought him temporary happiness. Through his interest in the Church, he sensed there was still a portion of happiness lacking.

MOSIAH 2:41: "AND MOREOVER, I WOULD DESIRE THAT YE SHOULD CONSIDER ON THE BLESSED AND HAPPY STATE OF THOSE THAT KEEP THE COMMANDMENTS OF GOD. FOR BEHOLD, THEY ARE BLESSED IN ALL THINGS, BOTH TEMPORAL AND SPIRITUAL; AND IF THEY HOLD OUT FAITHFUL TO THE END THEY ARE RECEIVED INTO HEAVEN, THAT THEREBY THEY MAY DWELL WITH GOD IN A STATE OF NEVER-ENDING HAPPINESS. O REMEMBER, REMEMBER THAT THESE THINGS ARE TRUE; FOR THE LORD GOD HATH SPOKEN IT."

Shaun: "I look back at my life and see what's happened to me; I couldn't have dreamed of it all. I got through a knee injury. Usually, coaches don't give injured kids another chance. I got a Division 1 opportunity. I got drafted into the NFL and made my dad proud. There was still a part of me that wasn't happy. I just didn't know what happiness was until I was converted to the Church. Getting drafted, having money—it made me happy for a short time, but it didn't last. What I learned through the gospel is that true happiness is with the Lord.

"While playing football, I never had an interest in the Church. My life was just football, and I did whatever came with it. I believed that if I lived right, I'd be fine. I was eventually released from the Steelers and went to Buffalo for a year. That didn't work out, so I came back to BYU for a coaching job. It was the only place I knew I would get a chance to be a graduate assistant coach. There was a long list of guys Mendenhall could easily have picked for his GA, but I kept bugging him. It took six months until he told me I had a shot. I just had to bug him.

"At that point, I still was not interested in the Church, but I don't believe it was coincidence that I found myself coming back to Utah. I could have gone back to Arizona, where my siblings were, or California, where my family is now living. But I came back to Utah. I didn't have a house there; I would just live with friends. I got into grad school, and that was a miracle in itself. I'd had a lot of interviews, and people always told me, 'Your GPA is just too low. We don't even consider it.' But for some reason, I just kept knocking on that door and waiting for it to open.

"I met a lot people through my grad program: Kelly Poppinga, Nick Howell [coaches at BYU], all those guys. They kept saying, 'You need to be Mormon.'[1] It was then that I finally asked questions. I was like, 'Okay, here is why I'm not Mormon,' and I would ask all the things that nonmembers ask: Why do you have the Book of Mormon instead of the Bible? That kind of stuff. I give credit to the people from my grad program and the coaches I worked with. They did a great job answering my questions. They didn't answer every question, but they answered enough to make me think, *Okay, maybe I need to look into this*. So, that's how my conversion started—just asking questions when I came back.

"One of my doubts was with the people of the Church. Some were so judgmental, and I used that excuse many times. 'I don't want to be a Mormon; people are too judgmental.' But I learned that if you're going for the people, you're not going for the right reason. Go to church for the gospel, not the people. I've met a lot of inactive Church members since I was baptized, and a lot of the time I've heard them say, 'We just didn't like the people we hung out with.' I'd think to myself, *Man, I hope I never get that weak*. I try to keep my mind open to the main reason I got into the Church—not for the people, but for the truth and what it brings to me personally.

"I also asked a lot of questions about Joseph Smith. Back when I lived in Samoa, there were a lot of members who talked about him. I remember thinking, *What a load of garbage*. People made fun of him, including my own family. When talking about the Church, we'd say, "That's the Joseph Smith church."

"Now, I look up to him. He's one of my heroes. I learned about all he went through, and I learned that it was never his church at all—it's the Church of Jesus Christ."

"Another thing that troubled me from time to time was that I felt like I was betraying my family. They were the ones who had taught me how to pray when things were going bad. My life had already been successful with my religion from before; why did I need a new one? I felt like I was betraying Samoan culture and traditions. But there's only one culture and tradition that will always be and never change, and that's Jesus Christ's. My Samoan tradition was strong and good; we were always good people. But there was something higher.

"When I decided to get baptized, that's what I ended up telling my mom. I was relieved that my family accepted it. My mom and dad came up for the baptism. That's how open my parents have become. Before, when we were young, they were more headstrong. This time, they said, 'If this makes you happy, then you should do it.' I think they're starting to see.

"There were more people at my baptism than I'd ever expected. The whole chapel was full. Academic Coach Jim Hamblin baptized me. He's the man! I had been close with Coach Reynolds as well, and he confirmed me. It's hard to describe how I felt that day, but the only thing I could think the whole time was, *Man, this is probably the best thing I've ever done.* I felt relief and peace. The emotions were so strong; when they told me to get up and bear my testimony, I don't even know how I was able to get through it.

"I wished my whole family was there, but my parents were, and my BYU family was—the coaching staff and players. They took a huge role in my conversion. It was a magical moment. I couldn't have planned it better. I think my mom and dad became so much more open-minded to the Church. I noticed them crying. I think they were impressed by how many people were supporting me in this. I don't think they understood how big my decision was until they saw that. Even President Samuelson [the president of the university and a General Authority] was there. He also spoke and gave my family a blessing from the pulpit."

Writing about baptism, Nephi counseled, "After ye have gotten into this strait and narrow path, I would ask if all is done? Behold, I say unto you, Nay . . . ye must press forward with a steadfastness in Christ . . . feasting upon the word of Christ, and endure to the end" (2 Nephi 31:19–20). Baptism is only the beginning, and then the Holy Ghost becomes almost a map for the rest of your life. At his baptism and as a new member, Shaun understood this concept surprisingly well.

Shaun: "It's weird: when I got drafted, I felt that it was the end of my road. For all the other kids who got drafted, they were like, 'My football career starts now, and I'm going to dominate.' To me, that was the end. I was so happy. It was like a weight lifted off my shoulders. I could tell my dad that I wasn't that bad; I got drafted. There was a bit of selfish happiness, like 'There you go, people. Get off my back now.'

"If it had been a more lasting happiness, I would still be playing. I was still happy and grateful, but it was a different kind of happiness. I felt like I had arrived, that I had finished. The happiness when I got baptized was a different happiness. This time, I was happy because I had received a lifelong guideline. I thought, *Yes, I got the map!* It was like the beginning of a journey rather than the end. I got the map to true success. I could be poor, have nothing, and be unknown to everyone else, but if I followed this map, then I had everything. It was a beginning. It wasn't like football anymore; that ends when your body tells you you're done. In the gospel, the game goes on forever. It's a battle, but I'm just so happy I have this map.

"My first few months as a new convert were in the middle of the 2010 football season—one of the worst seasons BYU has had since Coach Mendenhall took over. First, we won; we beat Washington. But then we lost to Air Force, and things got heated. I was sad because I loved football, but I still felt so much peace because of my baptism. Then we went to Florida State and lost again. Two losses in a row. There was so much stress; the coaches were wondering, 'What is going on?' We came back and played Utah State. People might have said, 'Okay, we'll win this one,' but that wasn't the case. It was ironic because I loved football so much, but I was probably the calmest guy in the coaches' offices. Everybody was frustrated, but I remember being calm. The Spirit was so strong at that point in my life.

"That feeling of peace has helped me a lot ever since. I believe in our Church. It's not easy living it, but it's worth it. I'm trying, like everyone else. Even though I still don't always make the right choices, I have a guideline now. Before, all my prayers were basically, 'God, help me be a great football player.' Now, it's more than that. I'm so happy there's something more important than football to me. Being converted is the best decision I ever made.

"Maybe part of the reason God put some fight in me is so I could fight for my family. This might be a difficult feat, but I believe part of my life's mission is to convert my family. I believe it can happen, but sometimes they're stubborn suckers. When I was first converted, I called my brother and sisters and talked to them about the Church. I think I was kind of forcing it on them, and I later realized that it wasn't going to happen that way. I just had to try my best to live the gospel and be a good example to them.

"Since my conversion, I've learned so much more about prayer, and prayer is something that really connects with them—prayer is so important to my family. I've learned that prayer is an art. You have to learn how to pray, and you have to know what to pray for.

"My aunt found out she has cancer a couple of months ago, and I'd been praying and praying that it wasn't cancer. A great friend of mine told me to pray for strength in case it was cancer instead. That was huge to me. I called my family right away; we had all been praying that it wouldn't be cancer. They were getting discouraged, and I called them up and told my mom to start praying for strength, in case it was cancer. They took that advice really well. They started doing that and felt a lot of strength come from it. They felt more peace when they prayed. It turned out she did have cancer, but she was able to eventually beat it. The power of prayer is amazing; you just have to know how to do it. And the more you pray, the more you figure it out. It's an art. I think that helped me get clearer answers too. Instead of praying for a certain outcome, I pray to have strength, whatever the outcome may be. It's been a huge blessing to pray like that."

I've called Shaun periodically to see how things in life have turned out. His aunt continues to be free of cancer, and his family continues to become more and more open-minded about the gospel. Shaun still coaches at the Naval Academy, which he says he really enjoys.

Shaun: "I love the interaction with the young men during practice. That's when we spend the most time together. I love to see them all progressing—physically and spiritually. That's probably one of the most fulfilling things I do, knowing that in some small way I might have been an example to them or played a role in their development.

"My parents are complimentary of the Church. They like how we focus on family, and they love how beautiful the temples are. I was just with them at my sister's graduation from Arizona State. I offered to take them to the Gilbert Temple and was shocked when they were like, 'Oh cool, let's go.' We walked around the grounds—it was so nice, and they were just amazed at the beauty. They're much more open-minded about things."

Notes

1. An inspiring video about Shaun's conversion story can be found at byucougars.com, by clicking on "Sports," "Football," "Roster," "All-Time Roster," and looking up "Nua."

Cameron Jensen

"Take upon you my whole armor, that ye may be
able to withstand the evil day" (D&C 27:15).

*C*ameron Jensen met *with me at his workplace in Provo.
He would take an hour out of his schedule, meet with me in
one of his meeting rooms, and then return to work. During
our interview, Cameron bore a fervent testimony of missionary work.
He was so convinced that any greatness he played with at BYU was first
caused by the fervor he had already developed on his mission.*

*Witnessing his certainty that the mission had blessed his entire
life caused me to remember an experience of my own. I hope that sharing this experience of mine will add to and further vindicate Cameron's fervent testimony of missionary work.*

*A few days after returning to the MTC from my father's funeral, a
doubt began to plague me. How would my mom provide for and take
care of my younger siblings? I was the oldest of seven, and my youngest brother, Cael, was just one year and ten months old. Mom would
have to go to work to provide money; how would she take care of Cael?
Being the oldest brother, I felt it was my job to return home and provide for my family.*

*Walking through the halls of the MTC one day, preoccupied with
these thoughts of returning home, I was passed by a teacher I didn't
know well. He slipped me a piece of paper but didn't stop to talk to me.*

On this tiny paper, it read, "D&C 31." I went back to the study room and opened my scriptures. What I read changed my life forever because it made me decide to stay on the mission. I'll share a few excerpts:

Thomas, my son, blessed are you because of your faith in my work. Behold, you have had many afflictions because of your family; nevertheless, I will bless you and your family, yea, your little ones. . . . Lift up your heart and rejoice, for the hour of your mission is come; and your tongue shall be loosed, and you shall declare glad tidings of great joy unto this generation. . . . Therefore, thrust in your sickle with all your soul, and your sins are forgiven you, and you shall be laden with sheaves upon your back, for the laborer is worthy of his hire. Wherefore, your family shall live. (D&C 31:1–5)

If there was ever a clearer message in which the will of the Lord concerning my life was more completely made known to me, I can't think of it. I knew I had to leave my family, despite their difficult situation, and somehow the Lord would provide for their temporal needs.

And the Lord did bless my family. Throughout my entire mission, anonymous people in our ward and community gave charitable contributions to my family, and my father's book began to sell extremely well. My mother never had to go to a single day of work. She was able to stay at home and raise my younger siblings.

While my mission led to financial blessings for my family, it was evident that Cameron's mission gave him leadership. His aura commanded attention. It was motivating and invigorating just to listen to him. He had a power in his voice I've always imagined Captain Moroni having. He testified that any leadership qualities he had developed came from his mission. Unfortunately, I never got to play football with Cameron, because his senior season was my sophomore season at Snow. My little brother Jordan, however, went straight to BYU with a scholarship after high school, arriving while I was at Snow. Jordan wrote to me about what he saw in Cameron. It is evident to me that Cameron had received the gift of leadership during his mission, and that leadership was now blessing Cameron in all areas in his life. Jordan said,

Coming in, fresh out of high school, as a freshman in 2006, it was immediately clear to me why Cameron Jensen's nickname was the General. He was definitely someone to look up to. His personality was contagious. Everyone admired him. On the field, his booming voice was heard barking signals loud and clear, but off the field, his quiet, confident demeanor was even clearer. He wasn't arrogant about any of it either. He just led with strength; he commanded respect. Off the field, he was as easy to get along with as anybody I've ever met.

During our interview, Cameron testified that he had developed this leadership on his mission. In fact, when I asked him to name a decision that made a big difference in his life, he immediately started talking about his mission, which he served in Rostov, Russia.

Cameron: "I'd have to say it was my senior year, getting ready to go on a mission. I wasn't the type who wanted to go on a mission because all of my friends were going, or because my parents expected me to. I didn't want to go just because I saw my brothers going. I had other options with football, and I really wanted to know if a mission was for me.

"I always believed in the gospel; it wasn't like I ever wanted to join another church or anything. But at the same time, I wanted to know if this really was the Lord's path. I was going to dedicate two whole years of my life telling people about the gospel. It wouldn't be fair to them, and it wouldn't be fair to me if I didn't believe it. I didn't want to go two years wondering. I really wanted to know for certain if I was supposed to go.

"I gained a testimony for myself, and it came by reading the Book of Mormon, fasting, and praying. It's fairly personal, but I came away knowing I just couldn't doubt it. That was the turning point. My testimony has grown since then, but that's where I really gained a testimony and knew what was true. I knew I had to go. I can only imagine what would have happened if I hadn't gone. I most developed leadership on my mission.

"It started by being passionate about missionary work. I was serving the Lord. I believed so strongly in what I was doing. I want to help my investigators and myself, but I also wanted to help other missionaries feel that passion too, and be the best missionaries they could be.

"Unless you've been out there on a mission, you can't really describe it. A lot of trials come, and those develop you. Otherwise, it's hard to get those learning experiences; rarely do college-age kids go knock on doors for two years in a foreign country. Those trials brought me to a new maturity level. I enjoyed it and wanted to make the most out of every minute.

"Many incredible experiences occurred during my time there. What stands out the most, as I'm sure it does with other missionaries, are those we introduced the gospel to, seeing their lives change for the better. Sometimes I think we take for granted the knowledge we have of the gospel, and what a unique gift that really is to have in our lives."

After Helaman's son Nephi finished a tough day of missionary work amongst his fellow Nephites, the Lord comforted him: "Blessed art thou, Nephi, for those things which thou hast done; for I have beheld how thou hast with unwearyingness declared the word, which I have given unto thee, unto this people. And thou hast not feared them. . . . And now, because thou hast done this with such unwearyingness, behold, I will bless thee forever; and I will make thee mighty" (Helaman 10:4–5). When any missionary takes the work seriously, the Lord promises to pour out blessings in all other aspects of life. These blessings came immediately for Cameron.

Cameron: "Out of high school, I had been offered scholarships by Utah State and some junior colleges. BYU and Utah had asked me to come and walk-on. I decided to go to Ricks College and play one year before my mission. While I was on my mission, I wasn't exactly sure I was ever going to play football again. My dad sent out some film of my only season at Ricks, as well as some high school film, and I started getting scholarship offers. When I got home from my mission, the next day I was on a flight to the various schools who had contacted me—I had one week to decide where I would go."

Cameron was recruited during that time by Oklahoma, UCLA, Arizona, Utah, and BYU. Ultimately, he accepted the scholarship to BYU, hoping a Church-sponsored school would allow him to continue developing the spirituality he had cultivated on his mission.

Cameron: "The maturity I developed on my mission helped me a lot at BYU. I had learned to focus and have a passion for what I was doing. At BYU, I felt that same passion about what I was representing there. I was representing the Y, and I wanted to represent that well.

I wanted to help my teammates understand that. It affected the way I played. My effort just came from a deeper place, a deeper commitment. I wasn't just playing football. I was representing my family, BYU, and the Church. I wanted to make sure I was never someone spectators would look at and say, 'He's not playing hard,' or, 'He's not playing with passion.' When you're that passionate, when you have that conviction, there's something different in the way you play.

"There were scriptures that helped me have that warrior mentality. I believe a true warrior combats evil and all the temptations around him. Nephi said, 'I am encompassed about, because of the temptations and the sins which do so easily beset me . . . nevertheless, I know in whom I have trusted. My God hath been my support; he hath led me through mine afflictions in the wilderness; and he hath preserved me upon the waters of the great deep' (2 Nephi 4:18–20). I just love that Nephi, a prophet, basically said, 'I'm not perfect, but I know in whom I trust. The Lord has preserved me,' and he just has faith in that. That's something that motivates me. No matter what, the Lord's there—just trust in Him. It's a message that has helped me throughout my life.

"Another scripture that really touched me was shared by Herewini Jones, who came and spoke to our team in 2006. He read Alma 44:4–5: 'Now ye see that this is the true faith of God; yea, ye see that God will support, and keep, and preserve us, so long as we are faithful unto him, and unto our faith, and our religion; and never will the Lord suffer that we shall be destroyed except we should fall into transgression and deny our faith. . . . [He] has strengthened our arms that we have gained power over you.'

"In other words, if we do what we are supposed to do, we will be preserved. It says that so many times in the scriptures. If we focus on choosing the right, we'll be blessed in all areas of life. Herewini Jones told us that if we as players focused on our personal, spiritual lives, it would be translated into the good things we desired."

Herewini Jones, a close friend of Coach Mendenhall, was a martial arts champion who was never knocked down. He confessed, in his own wording, that he used to be "one of the Gadianton robbers." He since learned the amazing power of spirituality and now teaches the gospel in prisons and jails in maximum security facilities. He comes and speaks to the football team every year as well. It was evident during our interview that Brother Jones deeply affected Cameron the day he came and spoke. Cameron referred repeatedly to it. Herewini not only provided Cameron with scriptures that fueled his inner warrior, he also told a powerful metaphor that Cameron has since applied in all aspects of his life.

Cameron: "When Herewini Jones came and spoke to the football team, he told us the story of Miyamoto Masashi, a great samurai. Samurai would compete in duels, and there was a long-time undefeated samurai named Shishido Baiken. He used what was called a *kusari-gama* weapon [a weapon that consisted of a sickle swung around on a metal chain]. Samurais would come from all around to challenge him, but they couldn't defeat him.

"Then came a new samurai, Miyamoto Masashi. He did something different. He actually went and watched Baiken in training. After only five minutes, he figured out how to beat him.

"When the day of the duel came, Miyamoto did something that had never happened in samurai history. Samurais had a smaller one- or two-foot sword they would use to end their own lives if they dishonored themselves in battle. This was the first time that smaller blade was ever used for fighting; Miyamoto pulled that out so he could use both swords. He wrapped the chain Baiken was using around his long sword, and beat him with the shorter blade.

"Herewini Jones told us this story, and then he asked us, as BYU football players, 'Are you using all your weapons?' It was such a simple metaphor. 'Are you true warriors? If so, are you using all your weapons?' Why go into battle wearing just a loincloth? Why not use every weapon possible? It made me think, *What are my weapons?* It was such an inspiring metaphor."

Take upon you my whole armor, that ye may be able to
withstand the evil day, having done all, that ye may be
able to stand. Stand, therefore, having your loins girt
about with truth, having on the breastplate of righteousness, and your feet shod with the preparation of
the gospel of peace, which I have sent mine angels to
commit unto you; taking the shield of faith wherewith ye
shall be able to quench all the fiery darts of the wicked;
and take the helmet of salvation, and the sword of my
Spirit, which I will pour out upon you. (D&C 27:15–18)

Cameron: "If I could give one message to the youth, I would ask, 'What are your weapons, and are you using them?' We need them all to defend ourselves against the adversary, because he also has weapons. He has multiple tactics he uses against us. He can make us lose sight of who we really are. The devil wants us to lose our identities—that God is our Father and us His children. I also think the adversary wants us to be drifters. That can come from not knowing what we want. He doesn't want us to accomplish anything because when we accomplish things, we're weapons. We're truly warriors when we're doing the things we were foreordained to do. The adversary doesn't want us to be warriors—he just wants us to be drifters. Also, he doesn't want us to serve or uplift those around us; he knows how powerful that is. Nor does he want us to be confident in ourselves. Lack of confidence can come from fear—fear of failure, accomplishment, and so on. He wants us to doubt, to fear trying new things.

"The adversary uses all of that. Those tools can get us at any time. But that's where the warrior comes in. Warriors combat such tactics and accomplish what they were put here to do. Warriors use all the weapons at their disposal.

"I'd say my biggest 'weapon' is treating people with respect, honesty, and integrity. Above all else, are you treating people with respect? Are you using that weapon? Do you spend time thinking, pondering over what you really want from life? Not many people do that. Your weapons could include Sunday School answers too, like praying and reading your scriptures. Are you truly engaged in the basics?

"Using all your weapons makes you a true warrior. Are you a true warrior? Warriors will have trials. They're going to have stripes on their backs and wounds from swords—like the stripling warriors, who were all wounded."

"AND IT CAME TO PASS THAT THERE WERE TWO HUNDRED, OUT OF MY TWO THOUSAND AND SIXTY, WHO HAD FAINTED BECAUSE OF THE LOSS OF BLOOD; NEVERTHELESS, ACCORDING TO THE GOODNESS OF GOD, AND TO OUR GREAT ASTONISHMENT . . . THERE WAS NOT ONE SOUL OF THEM WHO DID PERISH; YEA, AND NEITHER WAS THERE ONE SOUL AMONG THEM WHO HAD NOT RECEIVED MANY WOUNDS" (ALMA 57:25).

Cameron: "A warrior receives wounds from the trials in life, but no matter what, that testimony can't waver. The spiritual part inside can't waver, because if it does, you risk losing the battle. Keep your testimony strong, and you can come back with honor. You may have wounds and scars from trials, but if your testimony's still intact, you're still intact as a person.

"Those who believe in spiritual principles gain a warrior mentality. It came for me when I crossed onto the field; you have to have that in football. If not, you can't play the game. But you can apply it into whatever you do because you can do anything with that spirit. Obviously, I chose to compete in athletics; it was a great way to get that aggressive streak out of me. Warriors can commit their talents to a purpose. They have a vision of what they want to do and channel the gifts God gave them into that vision. I don't think having a warrior spirit necessarily means going out and hitting somebody on the football field. It's being passionate about whatever you're doing. It's understanding the vision of where you want to go. It all starts with, 'Why am I doing this every day?'

"You have to understand the purpose of what you do. That creates the warrior mentality; you know where you want to go, and nothing's going to stop you. There are a lot of people who just blow with the wind—not acting, only being 'acted upon' [2 Nephi 2:26]. Warriors, in my mind, are those who have a vision of where they want to go and are going to get there. Everyone has leadership in them, but too often they sell themselves short on what they can accomplish.

"At times, we lose sight of our potential, get distracted, and begin to doubt ourselves. We're foreordained to do great things. It comes down to accomplishing the goals we set.

"As far as my experience in BYU football, the warrior mentality is what drove me, day in and day out. It comes from a deeper sense of purpose. You play twelve games a season. That's it. Preparation for those twelve games drives you the other 353 days in a year. Everyone has the same amount of time to prepare, but what do we do with that time? This is where the warrior mentality is found. It deepens your commitment, passion, and drive. People like to claim they have the warrior mentality, but it's the time spent in preparation, when no one is watching, where you really find out who the warriors are.

"One of my fondest memories looking back on my career at BYU was against Utah my senior year. It was fourth down, and they were driving in to score. Rather than kick a field goal, they chose to go for it. I remember looking at our defense as we huddled up. I've never seen more confidence in a group of warriors than at that moment. I knew without a doubt we would stop them. They chose to run the ball, and we stopped them short of the first down. I'll never forget that experience."

Cameron was a starter and an all-conference linebacker all three of his remaining seasons. Over the course of Cameron's three-year career at BYU, he amassed 294 tackles, 6 sacks, and 9 interceptions. He became the only defensive player since 1977 to lead the team in tackles for three consecutive seasons. As a captain, he was also named the defense's most valuable player his junior and senior seasons. During our interview, Cameron commented that the reason for his football successes was that he was "playing from a deeper place." He explained that "deeper place" was love—love for the game and for his teammates.

Cameron: "Mormon is someone I really admire. His whole life was filled with war. He overcame so much, and at the end he taught about charity. After a life of war, he wrote an epistle to his son about the pure love of Christ."

Since he was fifteen years old, all Mormon knew in life was war. "And notwithstanding I being young, was large in stature; therefore the people of Nephi appointed me that I should be their leader, or the leader of their armies. Therefore it came to pass that in my sixteenth year I did go forth at the head of an army of the Nephites, against the Lamanites" (Mormon 2:1–2). Mormon adequately sums up his life with these words: "For behold, a continual scene of wickedness and abominations has been before mine eyes ever since I have been sufficient to behold the ways of man" (Mormon 2:18).

This continual exposure to wickedness and blood would harden most men. However, Mormon wrote to his son Moroni, "And I am filled with charity, which is everlasting love; wherefore, all children are alike unto me; wherefore, I love little children with a perfect love; and they are all alike and partakers of salvation" (Moroni 8:17).

Cameron: "The true test of a person is charity. I think that's what most don't understand. Let's look back in my life. I was a sophomore playing at Bountiful High School. There was a senior named Ike Morgan, one of the best linebackers ever at Bountiful. As a sophomore, I was there with my eyes wide open and nervous, and Ike went out of his way to help me. I learned a ton from him. Who knows what I would have achieved in high school or college without him? I watched his film and studied how he played. I asked him questions. None of the other seniors helped me like he did; they usually thought, *Sophomore, don't bother me.* I still remember comments he made that to this day instill confidence in me. I'm thirty years old, and I still remember his encouraging words. That's a big lesson; high school kids normally don't reach out and show charity like that.

"So I always tried to do that with younger players when I was a senior, knowing how much that meant to me. Later, at BYU, I always tried to treat freshmen or walk-ons like Ike treated me and instill that same confidence that he helped instill in me."

Since his time at BYU, Cameron made the Seattle Seahawks' roster as a free agent and played with them for a season. Cameron was sure of what career he wanted to get into next. He had found a keen interest in organizational behavior—what motivates people to work together in unity and with excitement, thus providing their companies with better work results.

Cameron: "During my time at BYU, I'd been introduced to a consultant named Paul Gustavson, working with Coach Mendenhall. The principles he was helping Coach with, about how to instill motivation in groups of people, really resonated with me. I wanted to learn more. I did an internship with Paul at Nu Skin, which set me on my path.

"Organizations are designed to get specific results. I love looking at that design to see how a company can get better results across all departments. This can increase employee satisfaction as well. I'm currently working as an executive at NUVI, and I love helping the company grow and the individuals get the most out of their work experience.

"No matter what kind of work it is, finding something you can take that passion, that drive into is what's important. You have to find something you can do with excitement. For me, it's just helping things run more efficiently. I take great satisfaction when I see numbers increase. I love the thrill of implementing a new program and seeing it benefit people. That's the way I now channel that passion.

"So it's not on the football field anymore, but I have goals. I try to reach them, and when I do, it feels great. I believe the Lord wants us to be 'anxiously engaged' [D&C 58:27] in whatever we choose to do. We have our freedom to choose what that is; He leaves that up to us. But He wants us to be fully engaged and committed. He desires us to have purpose and vision."

CURTIS BROWN

"I know the end from the beginning" (Abraham 2:8).

*C*urtis Brown is *a well-known name amongst BYU foot-ball fans. I'd watched Curtis play on TV and had been impressed with the warrior-like drive and determination he seemed to have on the field. I heard teammates talk about his intensity (like John and Cameron, Curtis graduated right before I joined the team). Still, the fact that Coach Mendenhall had put his name on this list of warriors meant far more to me than anything I had ever heard about Curtis. I was so excited to meet him, for Coach's opinion of him more than anything. Coach believed Curtis had become both a physical and spiritual warrior, and that was all the reason I needed to be elated to meet him. I was hungry to find out why Coach deemed him one of the spiritual leaders of the team.*

So I contacted Curtis. He told me he was living in Fresno, and I expressed my desire to come and interview him. "Wait, you want to drive all the way out here?" he asked. He told me how guilty he would feel if I did that; he didn't feel like he was worth an eleven-hour drive. I laughed and explained how highly Coach Mendenhall had spoken of him and how passionate I was about this book. He offered to have a Skype interview instead, and I expressed how much more spiritual I felt an in-person interview could be. He felt guilty making me drive, but I assured him that this was what I wanted to do. Thankfully, my wife, Stephanie, believes just as strongly as I do in the cause of this book, so together we planned another trip out to California.

When Curtis opened his front door, I quickly noted his intimidating physical frame but also his energetic, happy-go-lucky demeanor. Curtis's smile spread from ear to ear; that smile invited me not to be intimidated by his physicalality. Happiness radiated from him. His wife, Kim, was equally happy, though a calmer, loving happiness seemed to exude from her. Her serenity brought peace into their home. I could instantly tell that the two of them got along well. Throughout the afternoon, they exchanged a lot of knowing looks, smiles, and laughter.

As fun-loving a personality as Curtis had, he would lean forward and speak with focus when answering the interview questions. Intermittently, he would sit back and laugh while telling us humorous parts of his story, and then he would sit forward again and talk with focus and fervor for the gospel. I had heard that he was a convert to the Church, so I started the interview by asking him about his conversion story. This was the first instance when he leaned forward and spoke as a disciple on a mission. I could tell it was an important subject to him.

Curtis: "I had great parents. They raised me to be an example, and I think that prepared me for my life in the Church. I don't know if organized religion really motivated me when I was young, but God was always important to me. I knew that He was watching me. I didn't always make the right decisions, but I knew, eventually, somebody was going to hold me accountable.

"I went to high school in Palmdale, California. It was a small Catholic school called Paraclete High. I had a really good sophomore season in football, and I received my first letter from BYU that year. They sent a postcard with their stadium, and I pinned it up on my wall. I thought, *That's a cool-looking stadium, but I'll never go there; it's a Mormon school.* My senior year, however, Coach Lamb from BYU called me up after their Liberty Bowl game and invited me out to campus. I accepted the invitation. The coaches flew me out to Provo, and I committed two days later.

"When I came to BYU, my focus was on doing my best as a football player. I just went through the motions in religion classes. I thought,

Why do I need to learn this stuff? I soon found that the Lord had more than just football in mind for me. I met Kim my second year, and even though we only hung out as friends back then, she had caught my eye. On top of that, the athletic trainer, George Curtis, talked to me about the gospel all the time. He'd say things like, 'You're a Mormon in the making; all we have to do is add water.' I never really got that. I was thinking, *I'm a plant? Add water and I'll grow?* That analogy didn't click for me. But he'd always joke with me and often invited me to learn more about the Church. 'Hey, if you ever want to hear the discussions, I can line them up.'

"One day, I was talking to my mom, and she asked me, 'Are you going to church?' I said, 'Mom, all the churches out here are Mormon.' She said, 'That's okay. I assume the gospel principles are the same; you might as well try it.' She was totally open to the idea. Then in the locker room one day, I said something about religion, and Matt Berry, our quarterback, said, 'You can come to church with me. I'll take you if you want.' Matt was a stud; wherever he went, girls followed. I knew if I hung out with him, I'd have plenty of girls to talk to, so I took him up on it! I thought, *I'm going to call him out and see if he really means what he says.* I called him, and the following weekend I went to church with him.

"After that I thought, *You know what? This Church isn't as bad as I thought it was going to be.* I'd been thinking something totally different, so I figured I may as well get a better understanding through the missionaries. I reached out to George, our trainer, and said, 'Hey, I think I might want to hear the discussions.' Back then, I had no idea what the discussions really were. I just thought the missionaries would come and tell me about the gospel, and then I'd say, 'Okay. Thanks for sharing with me.'

"What happened in my life, from that point until baptism, taught me some of the same things you learn from the story of Noah's ark. Noah was a man who had been asked to prepare for something he'd never seen. He obeyed and followed the Lord, but the people mocked him. In a similar way, Heavenly Father was asking me to take a chance on the gospel, something I had never known before. I took the discussions, and the missionaries asked me to prepare myself for a baptismal date. I said yes, but I didn't want anybody except the missionaries,

Matt Berry, and George Curtis to know. George said, 'You have to tell your family.' I said, 'But why?' If I had doubts or something came up, I didn't want everyone to know that I had bailed either. I had told myself, *If I ever hear anything weird about Mormons, I'm done.* And if that happened, I didn't want people to say, 'Wait, why are you backing out now?'

"The night before I was supposed to get baptized, I called Matt and said, 'Dude, I'm freaking out. I have a feeling that something's going to come up down the road I'm not prepared for. I'm telling you, when that day comes, I am not going to hesitate to jump ship.' He asked me to meet him at the temple, and we would talk.

"He sat down with me outside and said, 'This gospel is so simple that anyone with a true desire can come in and be part of it. On the other hand, it's so complex that it'll take a lifetime to truly understand how beautiful it is.' He said, 'I've been a member my whole life, and I still have questions. But my testimony hasn't changed.'

"As he talked, I really felt the Spirit. During that conversation, I remember silently telling myself, *You know what? I can do this.* So after that, I called my parents and told them everything. They were shocked at first, but when they knew that this was what I wanted to do, they supported me 110 percent. The weight was lifted off my shoulders. I didn't care who knew, or if they made announcements or hung flyers everywhere. I was excited about my baptism."

Kim: "I remember the day he came into a room where I was studying and announced that he had been baptized. My friends and I said, 'What? You got baptized? We would have come if we'd known.'"

Curtis: "So like Noah building the ark, I had been asked to prepare myself—not necessarily knowing everything that was coming down the road for me in this religion. Noah was mocked: 'You're an idiot! Why are you building a ship when everybody else is having a good time?' And just like him, people asked me, 'Why did you do that? You converted to Mormonism? Doesn't that mean you can't do this, this, and that?'

MOSES 8:20: "AND IT CAME TO PASS THAT NOAH CALLED UPON THE CHILDREN OF MEN THAT THEY SHOULD REPENT; BUT THEY HEARKENED NOT UNTO HIS WORDS"; VERSE 18: "AND THEY SOUGHT NOAH TO TAKE AWAY HIS LIFE; BUT THE LORD WAS WITH NOAH, AND THE POWER OF THE LORD WAS UPON HIM."

Curtis: "So I started to think, *Why am I making these sacrifices?* The answer was simple: for the greater good. I didn't know what worldly blessings I was going to get, right off the top of my head. I couldn't say, 'Since I'm Mormon, I get this, this, and that.' I think some people look for that in a religion, but that's not what I was baptized for. I was baptized for the closeness I could have with Heavenly Father, and I didn't care what else would happen after that. I felt like Noah. He bought in and followed the Lord, even though he didn't know what was coming down the road.

"I'll be the first one to tell you that the angel on my shoulder doesn't always win. Still, my goal is to be an example—not only for my parents and siblings, but also to all who want to know more about the Church. For people outside the Church, my race almost makes my membership more interesting. If somebody white is converted, people don't think twice. But because I'm black, people automatically ask additional questions. I've been asked, 'Didn't you know Mormons were racist? They didn't believe blacks could have the priesthood.' I can't speak on behalf of what happened thirty years ago. I can't speak on behalf of anything in the gospel prior to when I started investigating and having true desires to join the Church. However, based on my own testimony that I've been able to build, I can say that for everything to be true today, it must have been true back then. My testimony is based on my own current experiences."

Because of his race and football-player frame (which stands out in a crowd), people want to know more about Curtis's membership in the Church. He tries to "stand as [a witness] of God at all times and in all things, and in all places that [he] may be in" (Mosiah 18:9).

Noah's granddaughters were among those who were left in the flood. They had married unfaithful men and gone astray themselves. Moses 8:15: "And the Lord said unto Noah: The daughters of thy sons have sold themselves; for behold mine anger is kindled against the sons of men, for they will not hearken to my voice." The emotional pain Noah must have felt, knowing that some of his family would be left behind, would have been incomprehensible.

Curtis: "Later on in my life, when I got married, my family didn't attend the sealing. That was tough, but Noah had it tougher. A lot of his family rejected him, and he had to leave them behind. For a while, his wife and sons and their wives were all he had [Genesis 6:18]. My family's situation isn't near as bad, and one day they'll be sealed to me. Fortunately, if they choose not to accept the gospel now, they'll have an opportunity after this life. But I made the decision now; why not take advantage of the blessings? Committing to the Church was the best decision I ever made. I've never committed to anything else and benefitted so much."

Family was clearly important to Curtis. Hearing Curtis's love for his family made me interested to hear Curtis and Kim's story. I asked Kim to share how they met. (Wives always seem to give a better version.)

Kim: "We met my freshman year. We hung out, but I had a boyfriend back then, so Curtis and I were just friends. Then I went to Dixie, and we kept in touch. Well, he would write me on Facebook, and I guess I wouldn't write him back, but I don't remember that . . ."

Curtis (laughing): "You wouldn't remember."

Kim: "He says I wouldn't give him the time of day back then, but I don't know. Then I came back to BYU, and one day we happened to park next to each other on campus. I said, 'Hey, what's up? We should hang out.' He said, 'Yeah, right, I've heard that before.' Later on, when I was finished with my classes for the day, I saw his car again and left a note, saying, 'We really should hang out,' with my number. He says he thought, *Whatever, she'll be too busy.* But he called me. I said, 'Yeah, I'll come over.' He said, 'What? You will?'

"We hung out every day after that. I was impressed because he was the type of person that always said hi to everybody and made them feel special. He was always thinking of others. If he ever saw someone bringing in their groceries, he'd go out and help. As we got closer, he gave my mom and me tickets to a game. At that point, she just thought it was fun to watch him because he was a really good player. But when we got more serious, my family really got to know him and realized, 'Okay, good. He's not just a football star. He's a great guy too.'"

Curtis: "I proposed to her at the Pizza Factory in Provo. It was kind of lame, but because of the timing of everything, it was the only way I could surprise her and also be able to share that moment with friends. We were sealed in the Oakland Temple on August 12, 2006, and ever since then Kim's been my anchor. Her commitment to Church principles and her Christlike attributes and nature have been an inspiration to me. We all need someone in our lives who inspires us to do more and be more than we are, and that's who Kim is to me. Our marriage hasn't only blessed us spiritually and emotionally, but we're now able to share those blessings with our children. My extended family has become more open to the ideas and teachings of the Church too. They may not be at the point where they're requesting missionary discussions, but they do mention, from time to time, their interactions with members of the Church."

The feeling of love was palpable in that home as the two reminisced and laughed through their story. I could feel how much they admired each other and enjoyed being in one another's company. Love in a marriage is the best way to preach the gospel, for as Jesus said, "By this shall all men know that ye are my disciples, if ye have love one to another" (John 13:35).

I wanted to find out more about the warrior in Curtis. I'd begun to see the spiritual characteristics that made him a warrior, but how did he apply his spiritual, inner drive to everyday life? This is what I asked him about next, because I knew Coach Mendenhall had probably seen something warrior-like in the way Curtis approached football as well.

Curtis: "I think I developed a little bit of a warrior mentality in junior high. In sixth grade, I was picked on a by a couple of eighth graders; they thought it would make them look cool. That didn't fly with me. I wasn't going to be somebody else's source of mockery. I thought, *I don't care how old you are. You're not going to impress other people at my expense.* I had to step up, so I got into some fights to try and defend myself. Did I win? No. But I wasn't going to let anyone think they could stomp all over me. That mentality stuck with me through the years, and I wonder if that was part of what Coach Mendenhall saw.

"Fast forward to BYU. I played my first year as a freshman and even set a BYU freshman rushing record against Utah State. But from the conclusion of my freshman year up to the fall camp of the next season, I had a really hard time with some of the coaches. I questioned whether I wanted to play football or not. Some of the things they did rubbed me wrong, and I wasn't sure if everything was going to pan out the way I had planned. I saw a lot going on that I didn't agree with. Even though I had seen some playing time my freshman year, I felt it wasn't the picture they had painted for me when I was recruited.

"That's when I started thinking, *When all of this is over, what do I want the end result to be? Am I going to let coaches be the reason I change my whole career, or am I going to find other people to fight for?*

"At the end of the day, I stopped playing for coaches and started playing for myself. That was the main reason I decided to stay at BYU. It's like the movie *Next* with Nicholas Cage. He can see two minutes into the future. Like him, you have to start analyzing the different paths you can take and what effects each one could have in the future. *What if I make this decision? What if I choose this? Where is that going to take me?* That's how I decided to stay at BYU—I could see what would happen if I quit, and that decision was going to take me nowhere.

"I'll tell you—I may have gotten the idea from a movie, but it's crazy how realistic that is. When you're younger, you can only play scenarios out for maybe the next thirty seconds. For teens, parents might be the only ones telling them what could happen if they make certain decisions. As you get older, though, you gain enough experience to know that a split-second decision can affect the rest of your life. Now I can play decisions out five or ten years down the road. *If I do this, what's going to happen a year from now? Two years from now?* And my mind just starts playing that game—visualizing the future. *What do I want the end result to be?*

"So I stayed on the team. I ended up having surgery at the conclusion of that season and would need to redshirt [redshirts practice on the scout team and don't play in games] the following year to ensure a full recovery. I was the only player on the scout team offense that had been a starter before then. That's when Coach Mendenhall came to

BYU and became the defensive coordinator. The starting team defense always practices against the scout team offense, so I began interacting with Mendenhall at the start of that year's fall camp.

"Maybe it was because I had been a starter the previous year or because of my experience in junior high, but my attitude was a little different than most of the scout team players. I wasn't the type of guy who was just going to take a beating. On the practice squad, most of the players would let the defense do whatever they wanted. The defense was aggressive; Mendenhall was intense. Some of the guys would throw us to the ground and whatnot. I would tell the players around me, 'Have some pride! You're just going to let them beat you up?' The more they picked on us, the more intensely I played. When other running backs carried the ball, they'd stop once the defender got in front of them and avoid the tackle. I was like, 'Heck no.' I kept running.

"One time, a six-foot-four, 310-pound defensive lineman got in front of me, but he didn't tackle me because he expected me to stop like the other running backs. I kept running right into the end zone, and Coach Mendenhall chewed him out. 'You're just gonna let him score? Run it again.' I thought, *Oh, no, you're not going to have us run the same play?* We had to run the exact same play over, and I knew that same defensive lineman was going to be ready for me. This time, he met me right at the line of scrimmage and threw me ten feet in the air. I remember just laughing because I was never going to let up. I was never going to lower my intensity.

"The week we prepared for USC, the coaches told me, 'Reggie Bush likes to cut back. You need to run like him to get us ready.' Our scout team offense was running the plays that USC's offense typically runs. Toward the end of practice, I cut back on our defense, faked everyone out, and ran for about forty yards. I was like, 'Holy cow!' I discovered a new talent and began to learn how to manipulate defenses. I learned that it's hard for linebackers not to run to where they see the running back headed. I figured out how to exploit that weakness and learned to make linebackers think I was running a certain direction, and then cut back in the opposite. My first three steps for any run play were the most dramatic, and based on the reaction of the linebackers, I would determine whether to keep going in the same direction or cut back. Learning that technique, my performance against our defense really improved.

"So I think Mendenhall saw all that, and me working hard and never missing practice. He never really talks much; he observes. He never said anything more to me than, 'Good work.'

"When I finished my redshirt year, ready to play again, I really wanted the number one on my jersey. The people in charge of that told me I would have it, but they gave me number six at the last minute. They had promised number one to an incoming player as a recruiting tool. I was frustrated about that, and I think Coach Mendenhall could tell. One day after practice, he pulled me aside and said, 'It doesn't matter what number's on your jersey. You're always going to be one of my guys.'

"It was that simple, but it changed everything for me. From then on, that was my mentality. It didn't matter what number I had. I would stick with six. Even though I played on offense and Mendenhall coached the defense, Mendenhall was *my* coach; I played for *him*. To me, it was more important that I earned his respect than anything else."

Kim: "That's a huge compliment from Mendenhall—he is not easily pleased. Even when he is, he usually won't say much."

Curtis: "I had learned several things at this point in my life. Being picked on in sixth grade was all for a purpose. Being in a frustrating situation with the coaches, at first, was for a purpose. Having surgery, redshirting, and playing on the scout team was for a purpose. Not getting the number I wanted was probably for a purpose too. If you have a firm understanding of Heavenly Father and the presence He has in your life, you see that Heavenly Father has a role. If you've gone through tough things, you might believe Heavenly Father has nothing to do with the struggles in your life, but He does. It's all for a purpose. Now I like to think, *Why am I being put in this situation? God's challenging me to grow. What part of me is being challenged? Is it my pride? Is it my strength? What am I expected to learn from this?* I know in the heat of the moment it's hard to think that way. Still, you have to realize that frustrating situations give you the chance to grow."

The inspirational words from Coach Mendenhall were the beginning of a successful career at BYU. The following season, Curtis had 789 rushing yards, passing the thousand-yard mark for his overall career. He led the team with six rushing touchdowns. Throughout the rest of his career, Curtis only got better and better. Curtis was an all-conference selection both his junior and senior years. He was a Pre-season Honorable Mention All-American and was even named to the Doak Walker Award watch list, going into his senior year. Curtis was a dual threat to defenses, often gaining hundred-plus yards rushing and also becoming a main target for John Beck to throw to as well.

Curtis and John became the first running back and quarterback duo in Cougar history to total three thousand passing yards and a thousand rushing yards for two consecutive seasons. Curtis was the first BYU running back ever to have two consecutive thousand-yard seasons. He finished with a total of 3,193 rushing yards, more than any other BYU running back ever. He had thirty-four career touchdowns.

Curtis: "Some of the highlights for me included the victory against Utah State my freshman year. That was huge. My senior year had some awesome highlights, like beating TCU at their stadium. It was my first time beating a ranked opponent, and that set the tone for the remainder of the year. And beating Utah at the season finale topped it all off perfectly."

Curtis signed with the Oakland Raiders two weeks after the 2007 NFL Draft. He was a part of their off-season training program for two months.

Curtis: "When I was in Oakland and had first signed with the Raiders, I had a lot of missionary opportunities. Other players asked a ton of questions, like, 'Man, how was it, going to BYU with all those Mormons?' They'd drill me with questions for about five minutes, and then all of a sudden say, 'Wait a minute—are you Mormon?' I'd say, 'Yes, I am.' I could see it as soon as I responded; they would mentally go through everything they had said, hoping they hadn't said anything wrong. I could see their eyes full of worry, thinking, *Hope I didn't put my foot in my mouth.* But it was good, because I was able to answer so many questions and clear up so many misconceptions about the Church."

Curtis didn't stay with the Raiders. He signed with the Cincinnati Bengals the following August and played in all four of their 2007 pre-season games. In the end, however, he didn't make the final team roster.

Kim: "When he first made the NFL, we were certain he was going to succeed. We thought, *Of course he's going to play.* There was never a doubt in our minds that it was our pathway. But things didn't work out. Now, I can say I'm glad it didn't. It's still tough because that was what he had worked all those years for. But now I can see that it worked out better for us on this path."

Curtis: "Honestly, it taught me an interesting lesson about the gospel. Of all the things I put my whole heart and soul into, there was only one that came through for me. I put everything into football, and it failed in the end. I didn't stay in the NFL. I committed to certain jobs, and they didn't end up working out. The thing that never failed me was this gospel. Being a member of the Church, this marriage, and everything else that Christ is behind—that has always worked to my advantage."

"All things must fail—but charity is the pure love of Christ, and it endureth forever" (Moroni 7:46–47).

Many sons and daughters of God have a warrior spirit within them, but few develop it. Few stand up for the right when it's hard. Few delve tirelessly into the scriptures, discovering and harnessing spiritual gifts. Children of God who really cultivate the warrior within them are perhaps subconsciously drawn to each other—D&C 88:40: "For intelligence cleaveth unto intelligence; wisdom receiveth wisdom; truth embraceth truth; virtue loveth virtue; light cleaveth unto light."

This may have been one reason Curtis was attracted to Kim. Kim was indeed a warrior. Interestingly, however, Kim's warrior side was not obvious until the last part of the interview. Throughout most of the interview, Kim had listened quietly to Curtis, rarely saying anything. As I began to direct some of my questions toward her, Kim's strength began to show. I'm not sure Kim even recognized the warrior within herself. It was interesting to watch, during the last part of this interview, question by question, how Kim revealed her strong and courageous side.

Kim: "It's hard for me to think of myself as a warrior. When I think of a warrior, I think of aggression. During high school, I never had any feelings of aggression. I just wanted to be an example. My friends knew my standards and respected them. They always knew where I stood. Wherever drinks were served, they'd always get me a Diet Dr. Pepper."

Curtis: "She was a leader for good in high school. In that way, she was a warrior. Kim proved herself a warrior in how faithful she was when we weren't able to have kids too. We tried in vitro fertilization seven times. I think one of the biggest challenges in her life, where a warrior's attitude really came out for her, was after the fourth or fifth failed in-vitro. It may have taken a toll on her spiritually, but she always read her scriptures. It would be completely dark in our room, and all of a sudden I would see her phone lit up. There she was, reading in the Book of Mormon. I don't know—how were you able to do that, Kim?"

Kim: "Well, I don't know. My favorite scripture is 1 Nephi 3:7: 'I will go and do the things which the Lord hath commanded.' I remember reading it in seminary, it being a scripture mastery. I liked Nephi's mindset, saying, 'I'm going to do whatever He commands me to do.' So when the prophet said, 'Only one ear piercing,' I said, 'Okay, I'll only have one ear piercing.' I just tried to do whatever He wanted me to do. In high school, I made the commitment to not have sex before I'm married. I wanted that so that one day, when I had kids, I could say, 'You can keep this standard. I did.' So when the temptation came to become bitter toward God because I couldn't have kids, I knew I had already made the decision to read my scriptures and pray."

Curtis: "That's what a warrior is: not letting yourself down. In this life of temptation, you have to drive the warrior within you to hold true to all your goals and standards. You keep them at all costs. The worst thing you can do to yourself is give up on the things you value the most. Maybe Kim doesn't feel it, but she's a warrior in so many ways."

Striving to bring a family into the world, Curtis and Kim began in vitro fertilization in the summer of 2009 and kept trying through the fall of 2011. Each succeeding attempt, doctors would tell Curtis and Kim that chances were high for conception and that it was an oddity they had been unsuccessful before, given that neither had any apparent physical problems.

Kim: "Many times, I thought that it would have been easier if the doctors had just said, 'You'll never be able to have children.' Then we would have been able to move on toward adoption. But they always told us, 'Everything looks perfect. This time, it should work.' But attempt after attempt failed. I don't know how many times I would have tried before saying, 'Okay, we're done.'

Curtis: "It got tough for a while. Taking a step back, Heavenly Father was definitely preparing us to be better parents. To be a warrior, you have to be pushed to the limit. You truly have to test your boundaries and get outside your comfort zone. Both of us were pushed to our limits, and our trust in God was tested—so much so that we questioned Him from time to time."

Kim: "It was confusing because what we wanted was a righteous desire. We wanted an eternal family. We thought, *Why aren't we able to accomplish such a good thing?* Our families were fasting and praying for us, so we thought it had to work. But try after try failed.

"People would try to comfort us, saying, 'It'll be fine in the end.' I thought, *In the end? So I have to go all those years without having a family?* It was frustrating back then because when you desire something so good, you feel like Heavenly Father will answer you more immediately. I wasn't asking for a new car. I wanted a family, to be together forever! I have to admit, I almost got angry with Him at times, but I never stopped praying. I never stopped reading my scriptures. When you want something bad enough, you just keep going.

"There were times I felt so alone. Curtis was by my side the whole time, but he couldn't understand what a woman goes through in this process. I felt lonely, but reading my scriptures brought me a realization that I wasn't alone. It gave me more peace. I could feel the Savior knew exactly what I was going through. Maybe He was the only One that would know. So even in my bitterness, the Lord still brought me peace through the scriptures."

"And he shall go forth, suffering pains and afflictions and temptations of every kind; and this that the word might be fulfilled which saith he will take upon him the pains and the sicknesses of his people. And he will take upon him death, that he may loose the bands of death which bind his people; and he will take upon him their infirmities, that his bowels may be filled with mercy, according to the flesh, that he may know according to the flesh how to succor his people *according to their infirmities"* (Alma 7:11–12; emphasis added).

Something happened in Gethsemane that gave the Savior the power to understand exactly what Kim went through, desiring to have children with all of her heart, being assured by the doctors that she could do it, but failing again and again. This feeling of understanding from our Lord was perhaps what gave Kim the strength to continue on in faith.

Curtis: "I'll tell you right now: As far as spirituality is concerned, she was the greatest example I could ever imagine. She's my rock. I'm the one always trying to keep up with her. I watched her reading her scriptures every night, going through something that was so frustrating, especially for her. I would pray, *Heavenly Father, it's not about me. Give this child to Kim—she's the one who's earned it. She's done enough for both of us. I know I'm not enough. I fall short, but please don't deny Kim this opportunity.* And you know, Heavenly Father did eventually answer our prayers, threefold. He made us wait three years to have this family, but we know that there's never been one time He didn't answer us."

Kim: "Yes, we've always been answered, 100 percent. It's crazy; we expected the journey to go one way, and it totally went a different way. But it all worked out."

The seventh attempt at conception, Curtis and Kim tried what is called in vitro fertilization with a gestational carrier. The embryo would be 100 percent Curtis and Kim's, but it would be implanted into a different womb. After much thought and prayer, Kim asked her sister, Jamie, if she would be the carrier. This final attempt proved successful. The embryo grew, and in the second week of October 2011, Curtis, Kim, and Jamie discovered a surprising outpouring of blessings. An ultrasound revealed triplets were on the way.

Kim: "From the moment that I saw them on the ultrasound to the moment they were born, I was overwhelmed with love. But it was even more powerful at birth. From that moment, I felt a new depth of love, and every day my love for them grows so much. Because they're biologically our children, the First Presidency gave us approval to be sealed to them right away. We were sealed in the Oakland Temple—same temple we were married in.

"The babies' little personalities are coming out so much now. They smile and laugh all the time. They're mobile and crawl all over each other. Days are busy—full of bottles, diapers, Cheerios, toys, baths—times three!

"Just to manage, I have to live by a routine and stick to it. They love being in their stroller, so every day we take a trip to Target, Costco, the mall, or just walk around outside. Each baby brings so much joy and happiness into our lives. I can't imagine life without them."

Curtis: "We had no idea this was going to be the path. If somebody had told us three years ago that we would be sitting here with three babies, we would've said, 'Yeah, right.' We had gone through fertility treatments for years, and we were finally blessed with the most beautiful set of triplets anyone could ask for.

"Recently, our testimonies grew exponentially with the news of Kim being pregnant herself. We just found out we're expecting our fourth. It was truly a miracle. Kim had been praying fervently for the opportunity to get pregnant on her own. I would cry myself to sleep at times just thinking about how much time and effort Kim was putting into her daily scripture studies and prayers. She was doing all the right things, and while her faith may have been shaken, it was never broken. Heavenly Father heard her prayers and gave us the biggest blessing of our lives."

Mosiah 23:10: "After much tribulation, the Lord did hear my cries, and did answer my prayers." Kim's story is a testimony that the Lord knows your fight and hears your prayers. He is close, even if you grow bitter. Many of His answers, however, come only "after much tribulation." Curtis and Kim learned this difficult yet rewarding lesson together as they waited patiently, and finally they were blessed beyond imagination.

Curtis is currently a regional field trainer for a pharmaceutical company. Kim is a registered nurse but has taken some time off to focus on raising the kids.

Curtis: "Kim and I love to take the kids on walks. The kids love their stroller, and if that's what keeps them happy, we are all for it. Our goals now are to be the best parents we can possibly be. We want to raise our children in a home cultivated with love for the gospel and for others. We want to raise our kids to have a desire to serve missions and share the gospel with their fellow men."

NATE MEIKLE

"And if a house be divided against itself, that
house cannot stand" (Mark 3:25).

*T*hroughout the course *of the other nine interviews, play-*
ers had asked, "Nate Meikle's on that list, right? Good." John
Beck, Bryan Kehl, Shaun Nua, and Shane Hunter all men-
tioned how much they looked up to Nate. They talked of his work ethic
and his resolve to stick to gospel principles, whether he was at Church
or on the football field. John particularly went in-depth on how much
he respected Nate—that Nate completely embodied the message of
this book. Given what I had heard, I knew this interview would be
insightful.

I drove to his Salt Lake apartment one day after work. As he opened
his front door, I noticed the same things I had with other players—a
husband and wife who were genuinely happy—but what stood out to
me and impressed me even more were their kids: four-year-old Kyla and
one-year-old Bennett. Kyla and Bennett were full of joy, and Kyla was
really polite. Nate, Keshia, and Kyla all introduced themselves to me.
Kyla had a smile on her face that showed confidence; I could tell her
parents had instilled a sense of self-worth in her. There was also a calm
feeling to little Kyla; I believe that feeling came because there was no
doubt in her mind that this home would always be a loving and safe
place for her. As much as Nate and Keshia's happiness and warmth

made me feel comfortable, I was more impressed by how their happiness and warmth seemed to make their children feel comfortable.

I began our interview sitting in the front room with Nate—Keshia went into the back room with the kids. Every few minutes, she would come back out to the front room for a while, listen, and interject a comment or two. Then one of the kids would call for her, and she would quietly exit. I began by asking Nate when his love for football began.

Nate: "I began to play in seventh grade. I loved and learned so much from the team aspect of football. There was also the challenge of doing physically hard things—things I didn't even know I could do until I did them. That taught me so much. For a thirteen-year-old boy, those practices were hard. But you never know you can do hard things until you do them. That was probably one of the greatest lessons I learned in my youth: When faced with obstacles, you can overcome them. And when you overcome them, you start believing in yourself.

"In eighth grade, I looked up to the senior running back on the team, Nate Garn. He was the best football player in the state, and I wanted to be just like him. One of the greatest compliments I was ever paid was when my ninth-grade coach told me that I had a chance to be as good as Nate Garn. That was a crucial moment for me—that moment when someone goes out on a limb and tells you that you can be better than you ever thought possible. In that moment, I started believing in myself and working as if it were possible.

"A few years later, when Nate Garn was on his mission, he sent me a letter saying he hoped I would break all of his records. I was floored. Though I looked up to Nate, I still felt a rivalry with him because now I wanted to be better than he was. I did want to break all his records, but he taught me in that moment that encouraging others is more important than any individual accomplishment."

Nate did go on to beat some of Nate Garn's school records, though he no longer remembers which ones.

Nate: "Beating some of those records was, at that time, a pinnacle for me. I've realized that what was really special about that experience was doing something I never thought possible, and it was in large part because of the encouragement I received from others, including Nate Garn himself.

"Out of high school, I received a scholarship to Ricks College, so I went to play football for a year. I was terrified, however, that the coaches had made a mistake in offering me a scholarship—I was certain I wasn't good enough to play there. But a week before the first game, I blew out my knee, and then went on a mission to Chile, so I was left wondering whether I was good enough or not.

"Putting football on hold was not easy for me. I remember thinking, *I should be willing to sacrifice everything for the gospel, but I don't want to. Part or most of me doesn't want to give up these two years because I'd much rather be playing football right now. But I'm doing it because I'm supposed to—because I'm commanded to.* I was having a hard time giving up two years; I felt that I would never want to give up football entirely for the gospel. But over the course of those two years, my attitude changed. I started to think, *I don't care about football—not in the long run. I don't care about anything I could accomplish by myself. If I can just help people have true joy and believe in themselves, I'm happy with that.* I'm still working at it—I, of course, don't have a completely selfless attitude. But the mission helped me get closer to that point. I became more concerned with how my decisions were going to affect others.

"While I was serving in Chile, my mom began to have some heart issues. Her heart would often go into vibrating mode rather than pumping mode. The doctors had to continually shock her to get her heart pumping again. She was in the hospital for several weeks, on the verge of death. Her heart just kept deteriorating. Finally, she called me one night and said, 'I love you, and I hope you stay strong in the gospel the rest of your life,' basically telling me good-bye. My brother got on the phone and said, 'Tomorrow, when the doctors come in, they're going to turn off the machines. They're going to let her go; she's tired of fighting. We'll call you tomorrow when she passes.'

"There aren't any words to explain how that felt. I dropped to my knees and started to cry. At some point, everyone loses a family member, and anyone who has will understand what I mean. So that night, I started planning on going home. I wanted to be there for the funeral and for my family. I happened to pick up a copy of *Jesus the Christ* and started reading it. I came across a quotation from Jesus in Matthew 10:37: 'He that loveth father or mother more than me is not worthy of me: and he that loveth son or daughter more than me is not worthy of me.' James E. Talmage, the author of the book, expounded on that quote for a few pages, and I felt like he was speaking to me. The thought crossed my mind, *I'm on my mission, I committed to do this, and I'm gonna do it. No matter what happens, I've committed to be here.*

"Whether it was the way Talmage described that scripture or the way I interpreted it, I just felt like I needed to stay in Chile, period. Some people might hear my story and say, 'That's a bad decision,' or, 'You misinterpreted.' The last thing I would ever want to do is make other missionaries with a similar experiences think they shouldn't have gone home. Different circumstances warrant different interpretations of the same scripture. But I felt that, for my own situation, that was the interpretation: *I've committed to this. I'm going to see it through.*

"I waited for my dad to call to tell me she'd passed, but the call didn't come early that morning. I finally called him, and he said, 'She's doing a little better this morning.' I waited for a phone call all day, but the phone never rang. That night, my dad called me and said that her condition had improved dramatically but she was still really sick. This went on for another two to three days, at which point my mother was placed on a heart transplant list. Just days later, a heart became available in California. The medical team flew to California, picked up the heart, packed it in ice, and flew it back to Salt Lake, where they successfully implanted the new heart.

"My mother is still alive today. I don't know if staying on the mission had anything to do with it, but I do believe in miracles—whether they are direct interventions by God Himself or just a natural progression of events that lead to drastic, unexpected changes for the better. But my experience in Chile (just being committed and never backing out) has paid dividends. Now, whenever I question my commitment to the gospel, I can say, 'I've already made the decision once; I'll stay on that road.' In the temple, I've made covenants. At baptism and during the sacrament, I've made covenants. I'm going to try to keep my word."

Keshia: "Now, Nate never doubts any inspiration that he has already received. He always says 'I already got an answer, so I already know.' I feel like that experience taught him to rely on the Savior, on faith, and on receiving comfort from the Holy Ghost during challenging times. Since then, he's never doubted a prompting."

Nate: "When I got back home from my mission, Ricks College had dropped all of their athletic programs, so I followed a friend to Snow College. During my first season at Snow, I split time at running back. I realized that I was good enough to play junior college ball but still a long ways from being Division 1 material. My second season at Snow, I suffered another season-end knee injury and didn't get recruited by any schools."

Though he was not offered any football scholarships out of Snow, Nate had worked hard in academics, even studying for a test during a pre-game practice.

Nate: "I stuffed some of my notes in my uniform and studied vocab terms on the sidelines—not a good way to fit in on a football team. I did fine academically in high school, but it wasn't until I got to college that I decided I was going to work as hard at school as I did at sports. I had an amazing experience with one of my math exams. I realized I could do math. In high school, I dropped out of pre-calculus because I didn't get it. I got a C the first semester and said, 'To heck with it.' But at Snow, I was taking this math exam and it hit me: *Wow, if I actually do my homework and learn the material, the exams aren't that hard. In fact, it's just the same material they already taught us.* From then on, I've been convinced that 'being smart' has everything to do with working hard."

Because of his hard work, Nate was offered a full-tuition academic scholarship to BYU.

Nate: "The dream was always to play at BYU, so I wanted to try to walk-on to the team. [It was then that Nate first connected with John Beck.] John was dating one of my best friends from Snow, Barbara Burke, and she put me in touch with John. [Barbara Burke later became Barbara Burke Beck.] I called John to see if he knew of any players looking for roommates.

"So John and I connected a couple times, and John was always kind and helpful. I really respect John. I just think he's a good, hard-working person. He treats everyone well. I feel like he really lives the principles he's covenanted to live. As I got to know him in a football setting, I noticed that he wasn't the type of football captain who was cursing to get everyone motivated; he was the one who encouraged people. He represented BYU well.

"When I first came to BYU, I was just a scout team player. I tried out for the team as a walk-on and barely made it. I don't think the coaches ever thought I would play. I made the team in 2004, and for a year I did nothing. I was just a scout team running back, so I redshirted.

"In 2005, just before spring ball, Coach Reynolds asked me to switch to receiver. I had never really played receiver, even though it was a natural position for me. At first, I didn't want to switch because I couldn't consistently catch. But I was backing up Curtis Brown and Fahu Tahi at running back and knew I wasn't going to play unless I switched positions. So I was forced to learn to catch. That's when I decided I would catch as many balls from John as he was willing to throw to me. If he ever wanted to throw, I made myself available. I had to make up for lost time. Before practice, after practice, and in-between drills at practice—if he wanted to throw, I wanted to catch. We always stayed after practice and drilled passing routes together. We worked together a lot. Over that time, we really bonded. I think it caused us to sense that we were coming from a similar place, both athletically and spiritually.

"Only a few weeks after the position switch, I became the starting receiver because the guys ahead of me got hurt. John was all of a sudden counting on me—he needed good receivers to throw to, and I had to be one of them. Maybe that's where some of John's respect for me came from: I came out of nowhere, in his mind. I was just a scout-team guy, and suddenly he needed me, and I was catching his passes. I was thankful I'd learned to catch in time. I hadn't practiced with John or with any of the starters the previous years, but I was able to come through for him."

Nate learned to catch in time to become a serious threat to Boston College. It was the first game Nate had ever played in for the Cougars, and he caught nine passes—more than any other player on either team. Boston College was only the beginning. Nate continued to catch pass after pass from John. He finished that season with 36 catches and 292 receiving yards. He also became a serious asset on special teams as a punt returner. He totaled 146 punt-return yards, including a 22-yard punt return against Notre Dame.

For the season finale Las Vegas Bowl against Cal-Berkley—a formidable team whose roster included Marshawn Lynch and DeSean Jackson (who both would later become Pro Bowl selections in the NFL)—Nate caught twelve passes for ninety-three yards. During his senior year, he continued to be a dangerous weapon against defenses, with 26 punt returns for 324 yards, 2 kickoff returns for 103 yards (including an eighty-four-yard kick return against Wyoming),[1] and an additional 304 receiving yards. Nate was named the All-Mountain West Conference punt returner at the end of that year.

Knowing what the other players had said about Nate and how much they admired him, I asked him next why he believed God had made him such a great leader in football.

Nate: "That's a tough question, because I don't feel like I was ever all that big a leader on the football team."

Keshia: "But he was the captain of special teams—[she then said to Nate] and you were voted into that position, right? Everyone wanted you there."

Nate: "Okay. I was a leader on special teams. Honestly, I just love football, and I care a lot about it. So that's probably part of why I was chosen to be a leader—I cared about it and the people on the team. I probably cared about them in part because I was the punt returner—I depended on them blocking for my safety. But I also just really loved my teammates. So yeah, maybe that's why they wanted me as a leader—I loved football and my teammates. And when you love something, you work harder at it and get good at it.

"I don't know that God necessarily made me a football player, but He let me develop whatever skills I was interested in. Because I chose to become a football player, He blessed me in that area and gave me certain responsibilities that come along with those blessings. Because He helped me to be someone who people looked up to, there was an inherent responsibility to be an example. More than anything, the two great commandments come to mind."

Matthew 22:37–39: "Jesus said . . . Thou shalt love the Lord thy God with all thy heart, and with all thy soul, and with all thy mind.

This is the first and great commandment. And the second is like unto it, Thou shalt love thy neighbour as thyself."

Nate: "First, love God. The Bible equates loving God with keeping the commandments [John 14:15]. Second, love your neighbor. That's fulfilled in part by being kind to people. So as a football player, it was important for me to be nice to people. I believe John was really good at that. Bryan Kehl, Matt Allen, Cameron Jensen—they're all kind people. But whether you're an athlete or not, treating people like they are children of God is one of two most important teachings Jesus ever gave. I try to always keep that mindset, and that's something Keshia and I try to teach—[he called for his daughter, Kyla, who was in the back room, playing] Kyla, come here for a minute. What's the most important thing in the world?"

Kyla: "Be nice to other people!"

Nate: "Thanks, Kyla. [Kyla grinned and ran back to her room.] I know that's a little corny, but that's the mindset we're trying to develop. Joseph Smith said, 'A man filled with the love of God, is not content with blessing his family alone, but ranges through the whole world, anxious to bless the whole human race' [*History of the Church*, 4:227]. That's the goal.

"When I think about being kind to other people, I often think of Todd Mortenson, a former teammate of mine at BYU, who later played quarterback for Jim Harbaugh at UC San Diego, and then backed up Tom Brady on the Patriots. I had just joined the team as a walk-on, and Todd was one of the first people not only to introduce himself but also to remember my name. I still remember walking through the locker room during one of my first weeks on the team, passing Todd, and hearing him say, 'Hi Nate.' I was shocked. Virtually no one talked to me in those early days (except John), let alone knew my name. Whenever I think of that experience, I think of something Johann Wolfgang von Goethe once said: 'You can easily judge the character of a man by how he treats those who can do nothing for him.' For me, that experience summed up Todd Mortenson. He's a guy who tries to bless the lives of others, regardless of what they can do for him."

In high school, coaches often try to get youth to compartmentalize their lives. For example, it's common for a football coach to say something like, "At church, they teach you to be nice, but when you step onto the field, you throw all of that away. Leave the nice guy behind. You have to hate your opponent." Coaches attempt to get youth to create a compartment, as it were, for the spiritual things in their lives. During athletic competition, they teach players to set aside that compartment.

Of course, when any athlete steps onto the metaphorical field of battle, there will always be a need to compete as intensely as possible. However, if gospel standards are compromised, and filthy language or anger or hate are used, the Light of Christ is also compromised. This indeed weakens the physical body. A true warrior can stand for righteousness whether at church, in athletics, in business, at school, or around friends.

While the people of the world seem to take on a different personality for each setting they find themselves in, "my disciples shall stand in holy places, and shall not be moved" (D&C 45:32). Captain Moroni, one of the greatest, most powerful warriors ever, never forsook his love for the gospel or Christ, even on the field of battle. He was "a man that did not delight in bloodshed" (Alma 48:11), but "he had sworn with an oath to defend his people, his rights, and his country, and his religion, even to the loss of his blood . . . and this was the faith of Moroni, and his heart did glory in it; not in the shedding of blood but in doing good, in preserving his people, yea, in keeping the commandments of God, yea, and resisting iniquity" (Alma 48:13, 16).

Nate: "You can't compartmentalize your life. At least, you can't do that in the long run and still reach your potential. In the short run, you can, but there will be consequences down the road. I believe in the law of the harvest—you reap what you sow, especially over the long run. I think that's something Coach Mendenhall taught me well; he always talked to us players about the danger of compartmentalizing our lives. I remember him saying, 'We are members of the Church, and so we're disciples of Christ on the field, in the classroom, in the community, and at home.' If we've made baptismal covenants, we are disciples of Christ as football players, or as anything else. You shouldn't compartmentalize spirituality away from athletics—if you do, it'll catch up with you."

MATTHEW 6:24: "NO MAN CAN SERVE TWO MASTERS: FOR EITHER HE WILL HATE THE ONE, AND LOVE THE OTHER; OR ELSE HE WILL HOLD TO THE ONE, AND DESPISE THE OTHER. YE CANNOT SERVE GOD AND MAMMON."

LUKE 11:17: "EVERY KINGDOM DIVIDED AGAINST ITSELF IS BROUGHT TO DESOLATION; AND A HOUSE DIVIDED AGAINST A HOUSE FALLETH."

Nate: "Coaches who try to get you to leave spirituality behind in competition are wrong, in my opinion. You should never try to be two different people, and you're only weakening yourself if you do. The more harmonized you are as a person, the more strength you'll have, right? Every decision you make that conflicts with your morals weakens your resolve. Every time you make a decision that supports gospel standards, you build discipline, and that builds strength. It's the law of the harvest—you reap what you sow, and if you're sowing good decisions, you're going to reap spiritual, mental, and physical strength.

"I've never believed the coaches who say, 'You'll be stronger if you leave religion behind during the game,' because I believe it's the opposite. You'll be weaker. If you're only religious in religious settings, you're trying to be two different people, and 'a house divided against itself cannot stand' [Mark 3:25]. You're actually weakening yourself. The more you can be in harmony, the more your whole being can be in unison and the more strength you have.

"I learned a lot from Coach Mendenhall's basic philosophy. He's all about consistency, working hard every day. He teaches his players to apply that not only to football but also to life as a disciple of Christ. I think consistency is one of the most important, underrated aspects of the gospel. Not that I'm perfect at this, but doing little things like reading scriptures every day has served me well. I've been blessed with a pretty good life. I feel like I'm in a good spiritual place because of consistency."

WRITER JAMES A. MICHENER SAID, "THE MASTER IN THE ART OF LIVING MAKES LITTLE DISTINCTION BETWEEN THEIR WORK AND THEIR PLAY, THEIR LABOR AND THEIR LEISURE, THEIR MIND AND THEIR BODY, THEIR EDUCATION AND THEIR RECREATION, THEIR LOVE AND THEIR RELIGION. THEY HARDLY KNOW WHICH IS WHICH. THEY SIMPLY PURSUE THEIR VISION OF EXCELLENCE AT WHATEVER THEY DO, LEAVING OTHERS TO DECIDE WHETHER THEY ARE WORKING OR PLAYING. TO THEM, THEY ARE ALWAYS DOING BOTH."

Nate's comment that "the more your whole being can be in unison and the more strength you have" naturally leads to the LDS belief that a "whole being" is not just a single person, but rather a married couple. The Apostle Paul emphasized this concept in 1 Corinthians 11:11, saying, "Nevertheless neither is the man without the woman, neither the woman without the man, in the Lord." Some athletes might believe that they are stronger without the obligations that families bring, but Latter-day Saints affirm that the strongest state of soul, body, and mind is that of traditional marriage. Furthermore, we believe that marriage is strongest and lasts forever when husbands and wives are sealed together in the Lord's temples.

Nate: "One goal of mine was always to get married in the temple. There was nowhere else I wanted to get married. To accomplish that goal, I knew I had to live worthily."

Keshia: "I think teenagers are faced with that a lot. At some point, you have to make the decision, 'I want to be married in the temple.' I had to keep that goal in mind constantly so I could be worthy to marry a man who could take me to the temple. In dating, your peers may choose differently than you, especially if they have different standards. Often, you have to be the odd one who's not going to the parties. You constantly have to make and remake that decision. But if you keep the temple in sight, decide beforehand, and just stick to it, you can make it.

"You also have to decide that if you make a mistake, you'll fix it. That way, you can end up where you'll be happiest. Making it to the temple is the happiest ending—finding someone who is worthy to be sealed to you for eternity. Everybody wants that in the beginning, but after a while it can get hard to believe that it's still worth the sacrifice. But if you stick to your standards, it'll be worth it in the end.

"And as far as our dating story goes, you'd probably get a better version from Nate . . ."

Nate: "I was more proactive in this area."

Keshia: "Yeah, he was definitely proactive. I was on the Cougarette dance team at BYU, and he saw me perform at a basketball game. He's told me what went through his head: 'She looks like a really sweet girl.'"

Nate: "I didn't see the type of girl who is into herself. I didn't sense the stereotypical dance girl, even though she really was a good dancer. I didn't even get to talk to her up-close that day, but I just got the sense that she was sweet and down to earth.

"I didn't do anything about it for several months. I just thought she looked so cute and sweet; I would occasionally see her on campus. One day, I was in the temple in Provo, sitting there and thinking, and I felt impressed to try and go on a date with her."

Keshia: "Luckily, he never told me that until after we were engaged."

Nate: "It wasn't like I was going into it thinking, *I'm definitely going to marry her.* I just felt inspired to do something, because after three months, I still didn't know who she was. I do believe the Spirit helped me, pushing me in the right direction and saying, 'Do something.' We had mutual friends, and I got them to set us up."

Keshia: "It took a little while for me to be sure I wanted to go on the date. From my perspective, I was just 'the dancer,' and he was just 'the football player.' I felt like that was too stereotypical. Other dancers were always hanging out with the football players, and it seemed so cliché. I was cautious at first, thinking, *He has no idea who I am. He doesn't know anything about me. All he knows is that I'm a dancer and he's a football player. That's a little too cliché. He's probably just a dumb jock anyway.*

"This was before I knew any of the BYU football players personally. It took me a little while, but my friend who was trying to set us up kept telling me, 'He's so great! If he were taller, I'd marry him. You have to go out with him.' At last, I finally thought, *Well, Dad's a huge BYU football fan, so it would at least be a good story for Dad. I could tell him that I went on a date with one of the football players. That would be worth a try.* So we started dating."

Nate: "And that pretty much was the end of it. That sealed it."

Keshia: "I realized that there was way more to him than muscles and football. I started to see someone special, and I didn't want anyone else to marry him."

Nate: "We got engaged officially on March 2, 2007, though we had decided in January that we would get married. We got married July 20 in the Salt Lake Temple."

Nate is currently working toward a PhD in business at the University of Utah. Keshia graduated with her degree in civil engineering and is now a stay-at-home mom. Their marriage has led to the happy family I found when I walked in Nate's front door. Having happy, confident children in today's world is rare, and Nate and Keshia must have worked hard to help their children get there.

Nate: "Parenting is the ultimate challenge, in my view. You're given this ball of clay and no instruction manual. Sometimes, this ball of clay lashes out at you or lashes out at your other children, and you have to figure out how to show love to each of them, even while one is hurting the other. In the workplace, you face challenges, but people are typically working together. As a parent, your children throw food on the floor to make you mad, or they wake up screaming in the night, and you have to help. But you want to help because you love your children.

"My mother had seven children. Whenever she would get stressed out, she would call her mother for advice. My grandmother's advice was always simple: 'Just love them, Jean.' Ultimately, I think that's all we can do."

On top of the usual stresses of parenting, Nate and Keshia have taught their children at an early age to read. Both Nate and Keshia attest that this is simply because of spending time reading with them. Nate has written his own book, encouraging other parents to spend time with their children and read with them. After the interview, I asked him to email me some information about his book.

Nate: "*Little Miss²* is the story of how I taught my daughter Kyla to read—at a kindergarten level by age two and at a second-grade level by age three. But I don't think my daughter is specially gifted. I'm convinced that others will achieve similar results when using the same techniques.

"More important, *Little Miss* is the story of why I went from reading three hundred books with Kyla each year to three thousand. Reading to children is the most important thing parents can do to help their children become readers.[3] And children who read the most read the best and stay in school the longest.[4] Still, 70 percent of parents don't read bedtime stories daily to their children,[5] and 40 percent of fathers never read to their children.[6] *Little Miss* shares the research that inspired me (some of which I've shared above), but it does so in story form, making the research more broadly accessible. My ultimate goal is to create a movement—to inspire millions of parents, particularly fathers, to read more to their children."

Notes

1. YouTube "BYU Wyoming 2006" for the highlights of the game. The first highlight showcases Nate's opening kickoff return for eighty-six yards.

2. *Little Miss: a father, his daughter & rocket science* is available on Amazon, either as an eBook or in hard copy.

3. Richard C. Anderson, Elfrieda H. Hiebert, Judith A. Scott, Ian A. G. Wilkinson, *Becoming a Nation of Readers: The Report of the Commission on Reading* (Champaign-Urbana, IL: Center for the Study of Reading, 1985). 23.

4. Keith E. Stanovich, "Matthew Effects in Reading: Some Consequences of Individual Differences in the Acquisition of Literacy," *Reading Research Handbook of Reading Research*, P. David Pearson, ed. (New York: Longman, 1984), 829–64.

5. "Harris Interactive Executive Summary of Survey Commissioned by RIF and Macy's," Reading Is Fundamental, Scribd, accessed November 5, 2015, http://www.scribd.com/doc/148798776/Harris-Interactive-Executive-Summary-of-Survey-Commissioned-by-RIF-and-Macy-s.

6. "Survey of Fathers' Involvement in Children's Learning," Fathers. com, accessed November 5, 2015, http://www.fathers.com/documents/research/2009_Education_Survey_Summary.pdf.

BECOMING A WARRIOR

"If you believe all these things see that ye do them" (Mosiah 4:10).

Something important happened my sophomore year of high school on Christmas day. I found a little newspaper clipping from the classifieds on the Christmas tree. It read, "Blaine Berger, retired NFL player—living in Idaho Falls—willing to train high school football players who want to play in college." I turned to my mom. "No way!" I squealed in excitement. Mom nodded her head, affirming what I hoped to be the truth. "I set up an appointment with him for you next Tuesday." I was so excited. Mom had always believed in my dreams, and now she was giving me the chance to accomplish them.

When I met Blaine, I was intimidated, to say the least. Blaine looked like the Incredible Hulk, minus the green skin: 315 pounds on a six foot six frame of pure muscle. I later learned he had played for the University of Utah and later the Arizona Cardinals as a defensive tackle. He made the NFL All-Strength team in 1997, bench-pressing six hundred pounds. The first day, he put me through a workout that had my arms trembling by the end; we tried to do some burnout pushups, and I couldn't do a single one. We continued training, and over the years my strength and speed finally grew to the point where I could play college football.

I'll never forget one particular training session. After having me do a set of ten reps with 315 pounds on the incline press, Blaine sat down on a bench for a second and just shook his head. I could tell something was wrong. "Blaine? Are you all right?"

"Come here for a minute," he responded, leading me to a corner of the gym. "Let's talk."

I'm not exactly sure what was troubling Blaine or what inspired him to tell me what he did, but it changed me forever. Blaine gave me a metaphor I've shared with every seminary student I have ever had.

"Brock, there are two kinds of people in life: civilians and gladiators. Civilians are fine watching the battles of life from the stands, but gladiators are never comfortable there. They have to stand up, walk down into the arena, and do some fighting themselves. You should never want to be a civilian, Brock. You've got four years to play college football—don't you dare sit down in the stands until your time is finished. You are a gladiator until the fight is over."

Blaine was of course relating the metaphor to football at that time, and it worked. I approached football with greater intensity than I ever had before. But I have since found that his metaphor relates to something much more intense than football. In this gospel, there are those with warrior-like potential, but they drift through life, watching others accomplish miracles. Some are content watching others testify with boldness and never wonder if they could develop that same intensity in themselves. Many "civilians" are born into the Church and live and die without ever finding out for themselves whether Joseph Smith was a prophet. They never find out whether this religion is all a lie or the most important truth of existence.

"Gladiators" have a greater desire to really know the truth for themselves. They do not let other mortals constitute their own beliefs. Like Joseph Smith, sooner or later they have to know for themselves and pray "with all energy of heart" (Moroni 7:48), "ask if these things are not true," (Moroni 10:4), and "[learn] for [themselves]" (Joseph Smith—History 1:20). Metaphorically, these warriors of heart take a life-changing step out of the bleachers and into the arena and fight the first fight for themselves—the fight to know whether this religion they've inherited from their parents is true.

That's why Shane said, "It was just deciding to decide. That's what helped me most. If it was true, I knew I had to do it [go on a mission]. I'm sure a lot of other people like me hesitate, saying, 'Well, I don't want to know if it's true, because if it is, that won't be easy.' But once you decide to decide, it makes the biggest difference. When I found out it was true, I knew I had to go. . . . There was no doubt."

Each one of the warriors in this book stood up and walked out of "the stands," in one way or another. They waged a fight of their own, down in "the arena." They were never comfortable being civilians; they dreamed of something more. That's why we've read quotes like these:

Cameron: "I also think the adversary wants us to be drifters. That can come from not knowing what we want. He doesn't want us to accom- plish anything because when we accomplish things, we're weapons. We're truly warriors when we're doing the things we were foreordained to do."

Carrie (Shane's wife): "I will not give up on marriage, no matter what happens. I will fight for what's important."

Markell: "We all want to fight against something. But the question isn't, 'What are you fighting against?' The real question is, 'What are you fighting for?'"

Kim (Curtis's wife): "I never stopped praying. I never stopped reading my scriptures. When you want something bad enough, you just keep going."

Shaun: "It was going to be hard leaving my friends and my sisters and brother, but I knew there was something greater out there for me. There was something beyond our island."

Shannon (Matt's wife): "When I think of Captain Moroni, I think of Matt. . . . But I don't think of either Captain Moroni or Matt as fierce men. I think of them as leaders—consistent and unwavering."

Andrew: "I've been able to learn what it's like to really fight for something."

Nate: "Every decision you make that conflicts with your morals weakens your resolve. Every time you make a decision that supports gospel standards, you build discipline, and that builds strength."

John: "I wasn't going to let anybody make my ship swerve; I knew where I was going. I wasn't afraid of how other people would view me."

Bryan: "With the gospel, it's all-in; it's not 'I'm a Mormon on Sundays, and after that I'm just chilling.' No, you need to make a decision, and once you make a choice, live up to your choice."

This is where you come in. What stories will *your* chapter have? This book was written for you youth. You must make your choice to get up and out of "the stands."

"The devil is come down unto you, having great wrath, because he knoweth that he hath but a short time" (JST Revelation 12:12), and that means if we do not fight back, he's won. There is no longer time for "lukewarm" testimonies (Revelation 3:16). Step into your strength. Become the warrior you were always meant to be.

ABOUT THE AUTHOR

Brock Lance Richardson grew up as the oldest of seven children in Idaho Falls, Idaho. He served a mission for The Church of Jesus Christ of Latter-day Saints in Montevideo, Uruguay. While serving, his father passed away from complications related to Crohn's disease. The desire to honor his father's memory has continually driven Brock to search for the spiritual warrior within himself.

Returning from the mission, he played football at Snow College and later at BYU. He met his sweetheart, Stephanie, at Snow, and they married in 2009. They have had two children: three-year-old daughter Kinlee and one-year-old son Kade. Brock adores his children with all of his heart. He is currently a seminary teacher and is part of a non-profit organization called Marked Generation, organizing events and seminars for children who have lost parents. He loves the youth and believes in the tremendous potential they have.

SCAN to visit

WWW.BROCKLANCERICHARDSON.COM